My sweet journey!

A Peep into the Past

Valsala Achuthan

Qurate
quratebooks.com

A PEEP INTO THE PAST

Valsala Achuthan

Published in 2024

© Published by

Qurate Books Pvt. Ltd.
Goa 403523, India
www.qratebooks.com
Tel: 1800-210-6527, Email: info@quratebooks.com

ISBN: 978-93-58982-69-5

I dedicate this book to my father, the late Kizhepat Sekhara Menon and my mother, the late Vadakkepat Leela S Menon. They were the ones who provided a good, memorable childhood for me. They were made for each other and showed me a life full of affection and sacrifices.

Foreword

I am extremely happy that my sister Valsala Achuthan is at present on the job of publishing a book titled "A Peep Into The Past" recalling her past experiences in life, which is a novel and fascinating idea. Since she is my sister, we had spent our childhood together in the same house, I remember most of the happenings expressed by her. We both had a great passion for the game of chess which was taught to us by our uncle, whom we used to call Kuttettan, just like our mother used to call him. We also used to have lively times playing other games, and many other childhood activities like stamp collection, coin collection, matchbox labels collection, music, etc.

I have gone through the copy she has made for publication and I can definitely say that I have not read anything of this sort before this. Her book has fascinated me and it will be the case with many of the readers, I am sure. I am ranking this book as one of the best ones I have ever read, not because the author is my own sister, but because of the way she writes and the creation of expectations and anxiety that made me impatient to know the contents of the next pages.

I wish her all the success with this project. Also, I am eagerly looking forward to seeing the finished product soon.

V. RAMKUMAR MENON

27 May 2024

Author's Note

There are umpteen autobiographies by various celebrities and successful people, but an ordinary person writing something about her past may be unheard of. When I wrote my first book, "Assorted Musings" my small granddaughter, Anushree, asked me why I hadn't chosen to write about my childhood experiences. From our discussions, she came to a conclusion that her life and experiences now are entirely different from the experiences of her granny. That was food for thought for me. Now-a-days children don't know how life was in yesteryears. This book is the result of that thought.

Probably, after my generation, no one will even know that the matriarchal system existed and also they won't know certain terms like' Nalukettu',' Ettukettu' and all that. Those who watch Malayalam movies will, of course, get an idea, but in the present generation, they prefer to watch cinemas of other languages, especially, foreign languages.

I have tried to express the various ways we used to enjoy, sans the sophisticated gadgets to which the present generation is addicted. My attempt is just to show the differences between our old generation and the new generation and make a record of a few events that had an impact on me.

Valsala Achuthan

CHAPTER - 1

Initial Years

"I do not miss childhood, but I miss the way I took pleasure in small things, even as greater things crumbled. I could not control the world I was in, could not walk away from things or people or moments that hurt, but I took joy in the things that made me happy."

- Neil Gaiman

Life is not a bed of roses, but it is full of roses and thorns! This is a known fact. We should pull out the thorns and make the way more conducive to our journey.

There is a general feeling that childhood is the best period in a person's mundane life. But children often feel that it is not so. From the point of view of an adult, everything is rosy rosy for a child. However, we cannot deny the fact that they go through all the emotions the adults go through.

Childhood, for me, was not totally unfavourable. It was a mixture of joy and sorrow. My house, or rather, my maternal house was in the beautiful town of Palghat, Kerala, close to Coimbatore (now, Kovai). It was a fairly big one, facing a small hill in the North, which most of the time looked blue, with traces of green. Sometimes, at night we could see it adorned with a small resplendent garland which actually was a wildfire. The same day, we could see her clad in different attires. There were paddy fields adjacent to our house, which became alive with the cacophony of frogs during the rainy season. That was once upon a time. Now, you can hardly see paddy fields in that area where my house stood. There are now, new houses and even tall flats just like any other city. My house, that is, my maternal house is also no more there. It was demolished a long time back when it was sold by my parents when they shifted to Chennai. When I was a small girl, there weren't any flats in Palakkad. The independent houses stood in fairly big compounds, surrounded by walls or hedges, but the people were very close and especially, in our area, the Koppam area, though the families lived in different houses there was a general feeling that all were part of the same family. People always rendered help to each other at times of necessity, but at the same time there was no unnecessary interference.

My close friends were Sakuntala and Jayashree. We always felt that we were born and brought up together. Since I was the only girl in my house, most of the time, in the evenings I tiptoed to one of the houses of these two friends of mine. Jayashree was also the only girl in her family, but later, her cousins came and stayed in her house and joined the school where we were studying- Moyan Girls' High School. We, the trio went to the Lion's Nursery School initially. If I were sick, Jayashree would also not go to school. Likewise, if she was sick, I too would abstain from going to school. Sakuntala had sisters, so she didn't have a problem.

We all used to walk to school in those days. There were not many cars and don't talk of scooters and motorcycles. Since Sakuntala's father was a doctor, he had a car. However, the children walked to school. I studied upto the 2nd standard at The Lion's School. By the time I reached 3rd standard, my mother decided to shift me to Moyan Girls' High School. There, since there was no vacancy in the 3rd standard, I was accommodated in the 4 th std temporarily under the condition that I would repeat the 4th std. Otherwise, I would not be able to write the 10th std exam since I would be under-age then. My parents agreed to this.

The Nursery school was a coed school. I detested going to school. That starting trouble chased me till the end of my education. There was one reason for this. My mom used to accompany me to the Lion's Nursery school on certain days while going to her stitching class. Normally we children were going with our maids. I had seen my mom talking to the teacher whenever she accompanied me to school. In the evening, at home, she would scare me by saying that she had spoken to the teacher about me and she had asked my mom to watch over me and report to her if I was naughty or disobedient! That statement chilled me and scared me to the core. The same dialogue was repeated time and again and I, being a small girl, believed whatever was told. After growing up, I felt that children should not be scared by the name of any-one, let it be a teacher or any family member or anyone in the neighbourhood or for that matter, ghosts or anything! That scar will remain there forever unless the affected party makes a great effort to come out of that. I didn't have any inclination to go to school.

Once I feigned stomach ache and the worried mom of mine took me to the Ayurvedic doctor nearby. He examined me and eyed me suspiciously and chewing his betel leaves slowly said to mom," Don't worry. I'll give her medicine. She'll be all right." I had to take that bitter kashayam reluctantly, but was happy that I escaped going to school! After some days, again I had that pseudo stomach ache. Again, I was taken to that senescent doctor, Dr. Seetharama Iyer. The doctor adroitly pressed my tummy just to identify the aching spot, but failed to spot it! Feeling my pulse and simultaneously spitting out his paan, he looked at mom over his spectacles and declared with a smile, "She is all right. No medicine needed. One day's rest will do." I squinted at the doctor, realizing that he had diagnosed the problem. My quick-witted mummy thanked the doctor and took the hint and led me home. A nonplussed me followed her. At home no words were spoken. It was all on my mother's face. At that point

I realized that silence can convey messages more effectively than a thousand words! With that incident, my feigning stopped.

I started going to school without much fuss. Once we reached school, we enjoyed ourselves. Along with studies, we had different games and a special PT period was also there when we were allowed to play in the sand, seesaw, apart from running and catching, and hide and seek! Now-a-days, where do children play some of these games? First of all, there is not enough space around in many schools. Moreover, many families live in isolated flats where there is no space for such lovely games. Students in some schools are taken to common grounds nearby to play.

The Lion's school had a big playground. Sometimes we would fall down, hurt our hands or knees or feet. The teacher would take us in, wash the wound and apply that indigo-coloured tincher with a piece of sterile cotton and that really, burnt! But that pain was more tolerable than the pain I endured when mom applied a 'poultice' on the wound on my knee. The hapless me was already in pain and this pain added to it. I hollered in vain for sometime and it slowly ended in a whimper. This was not a one day's affair. Till there was relief, applying poultice went on and I even thought that that was maybe equivalent to the pain a dishonest person would suffer after death.

Once, we all were playing during our PT period when suddenly one of our classmates started howling and screaming and we could see blood oozing out of his mouth. All of us children were stunned and confused. Teachers led him in and informed his parents (I don't know how because there were no telephones). The teacher must have sent someone to inform his parents. Immediately, they came and took the unfortunate boy home. Later, we came to know that he had a couple of broken teeth! It must have been very agonizing for him! Poor thing! Later, I thought that he might have got very much worried and pained and for young children such incidents are really appalling! However this boy, later, became a doctor.

For children, these are very depressive experiences. I had another experience which haunted me like hell. There was one Kuttibabu in our class who wanted to play the hero or villain and scare everyone.

He once brought something— a paper cutting tool which he claimed to be a deadly knife which could cut off one's head! He ran behind some of us, scaring us to the core. The teachers didn't notice this prank of his or didn't take it seriously. That night, I could not sleep properly! Whenever I woke up, I touched my mom to make sure that she was there to guard me!

Early in the morning, when my mom got up and went to the kitchen, I too woke up, and in my half woken up stage, I imagined Kuttibabu chasing me with that unique knife to cut off my head! I screamed, but my voice wouldn't come out. At last I managed to make a loud noise. Everyone came running, and consoled me. It was too scary to go to school, but my mom must have told the teacher about the whole thing and the teacher must have warned the boy and also reported it to his parents. There was no more trouble from him and life at that school went on smoothly.

Since the place is Kerala, we experienced intermittent rains. Sometimes it poured cats and dogs. Whenever it rained heavily, we found it difficult to commute. Mostly, our maid used to take me to school and bring me back too. Sometimes my youngest uncle took charge of taking me to school by bicycle, when he came down from Bangalore. We were very fond of that uncle since he was a very good artist and magician. We used to admire him drawing fantastic sceneries and animals and birds and what not! Apart from being a connoisseur of art, he was a magician too, captivating everyone around with his mind-boggling tricks! We didn't get an opportunity to see his stage performance, but small tricks like bringing eggs from an empty piece of cloth, producing flowers from nowhere, cutting a twine into two and joining these in no time without even a small mark, and the like were very easily done. He taught me some of those tricks later. I have never met a multi-talented person like my mom's youngest brother, Unnimama. He could repair many broken items. We looked forward to his coming again once he went back to Bangalore. He was a smartly dressed person who had a keychain hanging from his pocket and fixed to the belt.

During holidays, my father sometimes took me around to his aunt's place at Marutharoad where he had a lot of cousins. They all pampered me and entertained me since I was a child. There was a big dog which obeyed the orders of the people there. The youngest aunt liked to take me to the small tank in the compound and played with me, sitting there. By the by, my dad loved photography and he was in the habit of taking photographs whenever possible. I have a few photographs of many of my close family members. I enjoyed the trips with my dad to Kalyan Sadan at Marutha Road. My father's aunt's husband was called Tata (not remembering the famous Tata & Birla). He was in the police force and had worked many years in Tamil Nadu. Probably, the people started calling him 'tatha' meaning 'grandfather' in Tamil, but after coming back to Palghat, it became Tata. Tata had a prayer that everybody in his house, Kalyan Sadan, chanted together in the evening.

Once we were coming back home, to Koppam from Kalyan Sadan at Marutharoad on a cycle when it overturned while my dad was negotiating the slope near the head post office. We both were thrown out, but I escaped with minor injuries whereas my dad sustained a minor fracture of collar bone. People rushed to us, and took us and admitted us at the nursing home of Dr. Kesavan Nair, my friend Sakuntala's father. The accident happened almost in front of that nursing home. In those days, not much rush, and hardly any vehicle plied, except for one or two horse carts and cycles. He gave me first aid and treated my father and sent us home. I don't remember when my father started moving around. Anyway, after this incident, I had never gone with him on a cycle.

Instead of going by cycle, we started walking together up to the then Palghat town station. There was a Devi studio, the owner of which was my dad's friend. The main Palghat bus stand was also in that area. While walking through that area we could get the smell of coal. The trains were run on coal. No diesel engines or electric trains. I liked the smell of coal. We spent some time at Devi Studio and returned home the same way and dad would purchase a magazine on the way . At home, after dinner, he would open the magazine and my brother and myself, sitting close to him, listened to the story of The Phantom. These were picture stories. Even though dad was not an excellent storyteller like my mom, he tried to convey the story as interestingly as possible.

Now-a-days, children don't have that 'family time'....not much walking together, talking together and having food together! Each one is in his or her own world, browsing through the net or chatting through Whatsapp or Facebook!

Now, looking back, I feel that 'family time' bonds the family members together. We can discuss anything under the sun; Some can give solutions to our problems; We feel a sense of security.

"A family is a place where minds come in contact with one another."

- Buddha

CHAPTER-2

Trip to Pune and Bombay

"The best souvenirs from family travel are the memories that last a lifetime"

My first trip outside Kerala was during one summer holiday, when my parents decided to make a visit to Pune, where my uncle, Kochchammama, as we called him, was stationed with family. He was mom's younger brother, and incidentally, his wife was my father's youngest sister. They had a son called Rammohan who was two years younger to me. That was the first train journey I remember. There was no reservation and we occupied one full berth where four of us could sit. At night we spread a mattress on the floor and two could sleep there. My father could sleep wherever he wanted. I preferred to be with my father, for when everyone slept I got scared. Sitting close to my father comforted me. He was the pillar of our strength. My uncle came to the station to pick us up.

We had a gala time in Pune. My uncle was a Major in the army. He had spacious quarters. This uncle was very systematic and strict too. Whatever we took from one place had to be kept in the same place after use. He went for work in the morning and returned in the evening, after a tiring day. We all sat together for dinner and Sapota was the fruit we ate last, after dinner. That was the season for sapota. Every week, Kochchammama took us for a picture, mainly kids' pictures, but the attraction was the potato chips he bought for all of us. In those days, in Palghat, potato chips were not available.

As the army men had parties often, it was my uncle's turn to hoist one. We enjoyed the party. When the adults were partying, Ramu took me around the long verandah in his toy jeep, laughing and singing and screaming. Then we children played some games. My brother took me everyday to the nearby parks where there were many pretty and fragrant flowers. Our going to the park came to an abrupt end when one day we heard people shout, 'snake, snake'. We were so scared that we decided not to go there anymore. Visiting the swimming pool was also a new experience, but I could not learn how to swim! My brother did and he got opportunities to pursue swimming when we went to Cherpulacheri where there were tanks. I was overjoyed when I got a pretty doll which made a sound when tilted.

The next was a visit to Bombay where my dad's cousin was living. There also we enjoyed since there were kids of almost our ages. One cousin who was of my age had a master coming home to teach her. This girl was robust and smart, but she had the habit of slipping and falling down quite often. My mother was scared that she might accidentally fall on me and hurt me since I was a tiny puny thing.

We, however became very good friends and I was allowed to sit with her and take part in the learning whenever her master came. The master gave dictation everyday and we both wrote the spellings. That cousin had a habit of saying the spelling loudly and writing. We both got the same mark everyday, mostly, full when the master suspected that I was copying and he expressed that and asked me the spellings of a few words for which I gave the correct answers. He was so impressed that he told my father that I was very good at spelling.

We, all the children used to sit down together for food and the aunty used to serve us food. Along with rice, ghee was a must there. Then the other items. After food, we all played different games. The children preserved everything they got very carefully. Even empty biscuit and toffee containers were carefully kept aside. When we returned, we were given some of those empty, beautiful boxes which looked more attractive than the contents in them.

We had jauntings and outings on buses and trams there. They used to drink cool drinks while galavanting. I had never tasted bottled cool drinks before.

There were plenty of toys there in the house. The eldest brother or one of the adults operated the electronic toys for us. Since we were given strict instructions by our parents not to ask for those toys or touch those, we abstained from doing so. Many of them were mechanical toys and I was enamoured by those and totally forgot my doll which I got from Pune.

One day, I was a little sick, so I could not go with the others when they went galivanting. My father gave me company. Before they all started, I asked one of my cousins whether I could play with the electric train they had kept under lock and key, but my parents were very stern that I should not ask for such things which made me keep quiet, though a little disappointed. I was woken up from my slumber by the sound of some bells and conches from the next compound. I could see some fire-like thing and hear someone saying something and asked my dad what was happening there for which he did not give an answer. Later, when the cousins came back, I posed the same question and they said someone must have died there which made me wonder what was 'dying'! That word jarred in my mind, but I couldn't understand. Even though I tried to elicit the answer from someone, no one gave me a convincing answer.

For the first time I learnt that there is something called 'dying' even though I did not know what it was and how it happened and why it happened. Later, in our school text book there was a lesson on Lord Buddha. A lady goes to him wailing and requesting him to revive her dead baby. The Buddha's answer made me realize that everyone born would die.

Anyway, our trip was coming to a close and we started our return journey by train. In those days, if I remember correctly, it took three days to reach Palghat. No reserved berths. We spread mattresses on the floor and slept sometimes. Mostly, dad slept sitting on the seat for he did not have a problem sleeping. He could sleep anywhere, any time, any how! The only thing was, he used to snore loudly. On the way back, one old lady was asking." Have we reached Pattupadi?"What she meant was 'Katpadi' and unfortunately, the train had gone a long way from Katpadi. I don't know what happened to her after that! Someone must have helped. I don't remember the rest of the journey.

Anyway, the word "death" started haunting me! Probably, that was the first lesson I learnt- that death is inevitable.

"All that lives must die, passing through nature to eternity."

-William Shakespeare

CHAPTER- 3

Cherpulachery

"A grandparent's house is where cousins become best friends."

- Unknown

I hardly remember my first trip to Ramavilas (my paternal house), Cherpulchery. However, the first visit that is in my memory is the one I made along with my parents when I was around four years of age. We went there in the morning. I was a little apprehensive as I had no clue as to what would be in store for me! My achchamma was there and my aunty and this girl of my age. Both of us girls were a little shy and we began smiling at each other. Upon seeing our hesitance, my parents and aunt told us to go and play together.

At that moment, Devi and I became friends. We talked to each other and played. Suddenly, upon remembering something, she said, "I'll show you something." We tiptoed to the bedroom, and there I saw a cloth cradle, suspended from the ceiling by a hook. She slightly opened one part of it and what did I see there? A small, cute baby was laying there, sleeping blissfully. I was so excited that I shouted with joy, causing the baby to open his tiny eyes and begin wailing. Immediately, Devi started rocking the cradle to make him go back to sleep. Hearing the baby cry, my aunt rushed in, taking him in her arms to pacify him.

I enjoyed playing with the baby till we returned to Palakkad.

My Paternal Family

RAMAVILAS

My Paternal grand parents

Life went on as usual intermingled with happiness and sorrow, anxiety and relief till summer holidays. April and May months were holidays for all schools in Kerala. My brother and I used to wait for March 31 to get ready to go to our father's place at Cherpulachery. Since we belong to the Nair community, we were following a matriarchal system. Mostly, ladies stayed in their own houses with their husband and children unless the husband was employed elsewhere. In that case, she went away from that house and stayed with her husband. This matriarchal system was good, for ladies had a sense of security. In those days torture by the in laws was unheard of in such families. Of course, there were some drawbacks to this system too! My parents were at this house (Lakshmi Vilas) most of their married life.

Long back, as he started his career, my father was working at the ordinance factory at Jabalpur and my mother had gone with him. When there was retrenchment after the world war, he lost his job and had to return to Kerala. That's why we were staying at my mother's house. Moreover, mom's brothers except one were all outside Kerala because of their jobs. One uncle, who was a bachelor was staying with us. He was earlier working at Malampuzha.

Now, coming back to our holidays. March 31st, we rejoiced, for the next day we would be at our father's house at Cherpulachery, enjoying with our cousins. Uncle Kuttyettan would stay at Palghat itself since he had a job. When we went to Cherpulachery, our maid, Chinna's family, came and took care of our house. Chinna's daughter came early and played with us. The rest of her family would come one by one early the next morning. That night, mother would not prepare any curry. My father used to go to one of the restaurants and bring a big vessel of very tasty chicken curry to have with rice. At night, after dinner all the vessels would be cleaned, things would be arranged and kept intact. My mom used to give some rice and also money for Chinna's family to be used.

Chinna and family were allowed to use the side room with a slanting roof and also the wide verandah outside where there was a grinding stone and a stone mortar. In those days no kerosene stove or gas stove. We had to use the earthen stove which was lit using twigs and wood. Since there were trees in the compound there was no problem for them to get fuel. My uncle, Kuttyettan, went to the office in the morning and had breakfast and lunch at the canteen when we were away. In the night, our maid's husband brought dinner from a nearby shop. Chinna and family cooked their own food.

On April 1st, we had to get up very early. My normal wake up time was 9 am since we had school only at 10 am. However, that day, we had to catch the earliest bus to Cherpulachery. The previous evening, my father had to go to Muthu, the horse cart driver, to tell him to come early the next morning to pick us up. Our big trunk, my mother and myself could be accommodated in the cart. My father and brother walked to the bus stop. Even though I was feeling sleepy, I tried to keep my eyes wide open. Muthu made some noise to direct the horse, occasionally wielding his whip, and the sound of saddle bells chiming was like a lullaby for me, but I tried to shake myself off my sleep and tried keeping my eyes open till the trotting horse stopped at the bus stand. I can't explain that excitement and happiness! We used to board the bus well in advance.

I always sat next to my father. The conductor had noticed us whenever we went to Cherpulchery and he remembered my dad and always addressed him as 'Sekharaettan' as many people used to. With a smile, the conductor would give me the tickets. In those days, there were not so many buses and the conductors could recognize many commuters. The name written on the bus was Mayilvaahanam. Eventually, Mayilvaahanam would start slowly, coughing and sighing like a sick person, moving forward, negotiating turns and stopping here and there to allow people to board and a few to get down. The conductor, looking very pious with his neatly combed hair and resplendent face with one finger thick sacred ash smeared on his forehead, sounded the bell once to stop and twice to give a hint to the driver to start the bus and, with a whistle blow, said, "Right, right" in a sing song tone.

I liked humming while travelling by bus. According to the sound of the engine, my humming also went up and down. At the start of the journey, there would be darkness all around. Slowly, as the sun started peeping through the clouds, the orangish light would start spreading in the sky behind, for the bus had been going to the western side. I would look at the orangish light slowly turning into a bright day light, shedding all the beauty and charm of the colour! At the same time, the thoughts of reaching our destination would fill all of us with exuberance and joy.

There was a break in the journey at Kongad. There, at a small tea shop, the driver and conductor would have their breakfast and then happily board the bus. The journey would go on with me trying to catch a nap but failing miserably. When the creeping, coughing bus slowly reached Cherpulcherry the whole ambience would have changed. Initially, the bus had to go past the dinky bus stand where there was not enough space to park two buses at a time, and it would move forward to stop at the elementary school and take an about turn to go back. My father's house was close to the elementary school, so my cousins along with a lackey would be waiting there for us. The lackey, after bringing the trunk down from the top of the bus, would lead the way, followed by us talking and giggling with happiness. From the gate, we could see our grandma, aunt and uncle standing on the wide veranda of Ramavilas, welcoming us with smiling faces. This was the usual experience.

After our ablutions and breakfast, the time to rejoice started. Devi, my cousin, was my age. The eldest one is Maliniedathy. She is of my brother's age- five years older than us. Then, Radhikedathy, three years elder to us and the last one is Unni-two years younger to us. Devi and myself were very close and we played together most of the time. We had our favourite mango tree to perch on. Maliniedathy had a slight problem with her leg. Her father bought a rickshaw for her sake. One man was appointed to take her to school & bring her back from school in the rickshaw. She had special footwear too. Devi was a good athlete. I had seen her practise High Jump at home. But summer was the time to relax.

In the summer breeze, one mango tree would drop mangoes whenever it felt like doing so. We the kids collected the mangoes and the poor children of the neighbouring house also joined us in collecting those pulimango, as we called it! Later only I came to know that those mangoes were the only lunch those kids had on certain days. Sometimes, granny gave them food. Feeding them everyday was not practical. They were at liberty to collect wood from the compound, pluck drumstick leaves, collect gooseberries etc.

We roamed around the compound like the liberated cows, however, we abstained from going to the end of the compound wall, for someone had committed suicide on a branch of a cashewnut tree there. Yet another piece of knowledge for a small girl. Apart from dying, people might commit suicide too!

The compound was of four acres and it was full of mango trees, jackfruit trees, cashewnut trees and one or two sapota, jamun, coconut and some other trees. These trees had been planted in a very systematic way, with enough vacant space in between. My paternal grandfather who was a district judge, after retirement, bought this land with my granny's share money and constructed this big house and planted those trees. He was very sure that he wouldn't reap the fruits of his work. But he wanted his children and grandchildren to enjoy it. This particular place had witnessed many joys and sorrows.

I will talk about it later. Life is a mixture of both!

We, children, one day would put up a show for the elders to witness. After so many days' of practice, we danced, sang and did so many other things to entertain them. There was a small bathroom covered with a foldable stand. That was our dressing room if anyone wanted to change her costume. The room would be decorated with mango leaf hangings and flowers. The children as well as the adults enjoyed the programme!

During summer holidays, after lunch, granny (achchamma) used to give us goodies like cashew nuts and jackfruit jam prepared by her! Then, after the school exam results came, since all of us would pass, granny would make her special egg curry for lunch! How delicious her preparations were!

Achamma prepared a special item, a confection, an electuary with gooseberries which has medicinal value.

She had a small brass box (chella petti) in which she used to keep betel leaves. After lunch and dinner, she ate a leaf. First, she would snip off the small stem, wipe the leaf with a cloth and apply shell lime paste and pieces of betel nut, fold it and put it in her mouth. Her lips always had that reddish tinge and her breath had the smell of scented arecanut. She was a very soft-spoken lady. Whenever I got time, I observed her.

Devi and I used to sit on our favourite mango tree whenever possible. We could see a few big ants going in lines through these mango trees. At Palghat, I had never seen such big red ants! The spiders were also big. Even the colour of the soil was different! At Cherpulachery, the soil was reddish in colour, but at Palghat it was the colour of sand.

At Ramavilas, in the morning and at dusk, achamma lit the sacred lamp. Normally, one of my cousins took the lamp around, but as long as I was there, I took the responsibility of taking the lamp around. Devi accompanied me, giving instructions. First, the lit lamp had to be taken to the front verandah,to show it to the gate side. The gate was a little away from the main house. Then it should be taken to the other verandah, on the eastern side and shown to the cows in the cow shed. After that it was taken to the Tulsi thara. We didn't go near it, but placed the wick on the steps of the house facing the thara. At last the lamp had to be brought to the western side where a few photos of God were placed. This was the usual procedure. Then we children went to the prayer room and chanted slokas mostly in unison. We started with 'Namah Shivaya...' followed by 'ennunni krishna', 'onnam thruppadi', 'Radha Ramana' etc. There was no particular order. Then aunty went, followed by Devi's father. His 'interaction' with God was a little long. Devi's father was very pious. Going to the prayer room and chanting slokas together was like a psychological treatment. My parents never chanted like this. In fact, my father did not believe in rituals, or horoscopes, and he did not go to temples to worship. He never used to adorn his forehead with the sacred ash or chandan. However, he believed in one supreme being. Dad liked to chant a couple of slokas like "Aaigiri Nandini" and "Bhajagovindam" etc. whenever he was relaxing. He never prayed for anything.

Devi's dad made Pulimughathu Panickar come home often to know what, I am not very sure. A couple of times, when I was there the Panicker came in the morning with a bag filled with a board or chart and cowrie shells and other paraphernalia. I had seen him only once or twice. As soon as he came, he washed his feet with the water kept in a special brass vessel called 'kindi', adjusted his dhoti, covering his upper body and walked upstairs with uncle. His forehead was smeared with sacred ash. Very cautiously, he climbed the wooden stairs with uncle. I was told that he used to visit Ramavilas and the houses of our relatives often and I wondered whether he would predict different things each time he came. Anyway, after his work and prediction, he would go away happily, accepting the Dakshina. People of that area had faith in his predictions.

Granny prayed for quite some time in the morning and also at dusk. In the morning she kept a small dish of malar as prasad. That was for me whenever I was there. After bath and her long morning prayers, achamma wrote 'Sri Rama Jayam' in a book for some time. Then she fed the crows and after that, fed herself.

Devi's dad was a very mild person and he was very systematic. In the mornings, he preferred to have idly or dosa with fried onion chutney which was very tasty. He was a good conversationalist and he was a learned man, jovial and had a kind disposition. He used to say, "Girish" every now and then. I think he liked that name very much.

Myself and Devi

Jackfruit tree

Devi and I had gone with granny to the Ayyappan temple a few times for sapthaham by Anjam Namboodiri. I was introduced to spirituality then, I should say. We three used to walk to the temple. We looked at our granny as someone who was good at solving everybody's problems. Achamma had some quick remedies if anyone fell sick. Some of us used to develop a headache at times. She would make a paste of pepper, put it in buttermilk, boil it and make a thick paste, spread it on a piece of cloth and put that cloth on the patient's forehead. Very soon the patient would get up relieved and smiling and declaring," poyi poche, poyinthi, poyallo" etc. She had remedies for other problems too.

If anyone lost something, granny would ask that person to pray to God and say, "If I get that back, I would organize a kottum chiriyum." Actually, I didn't believe this initially, but then, I misplaced something I liked very much. Achamma told me to pray to God and do this. I did, and within a couple of days, I got it back! That evening, we girls sat around the dining table. A copper vessel, full of water, was kept on the table. Five wicks were lit and we all clapped our hands and laughed loudly for some time. The prasad prepared with roasted rice, jaggery and grated coconut was kept near the copper vessel. We ate the prasad. It was an amusing custom!

Some years, dad's other sister, Meenucheriamma and family came down to Ramavilas from Bombay. Sometimes dad's brother whom we called Valiya Unnimama and family came. This didn't happen every year. Those days, travelling was a little tedious.

Meenucheriamma's daughter, Lata, was a good singer. She used to sing like Latha Mangeshkar. She was very talented. Lata was good at stitching and whenever she came to Ramavilas, she helped Kunhilakshmi, the maid, clean the house. Her brother, Ramdas was a brilliant boy. Unnimama and Radhammayi had three children. They were much younger to us. Those three children, Satish, Suresh and Sumi were very cute and we girls took turns to carry them around.

When so many of us got together, we had great fun. We children used to go trekking to the small hill which was behind Ramavilas. Some days some grown ups also accompanied us. On our way back, sometimes we girls used to go to the small temple on the slopes of the hill. The oracle of that small temple was one of the maid's mothers working at Ramavilas.

Certain years, during summer, there was scarcity of water, especially if the members were more in number. At Palghat, the Municipality supplied water in lorries, but in Cherpalchery, it was not possible. Achamma arranged for a few people to bring water from a neighbouring house which had a deep well, full of water. In Palghat, the problem was solved once the government started supplying Malampuzha water through pipes.

Another attraction at Cherpulchery was our going to Devi's father's house. It was a little away from Ramavilas, but we went on foot. Through the narrow, winding road we walked and walked, Devi showing me the small temple on top of a small hill, a puddle that never dried up etc. Talking, we used to walk, enjoying the beauty and quietness of nature. Once we reached Matom, we joined the other children there and played, went to the pool, sat in the padippura and talked and played. Sometimes the elephant of Cherpulachery temple was brought there and tied in the big backyard.

The mahout took the tusker every evening to the pool to give it a bath and on its way to the pool, we children gave it jaggery, plantain and pieces of coconut which he relished. Both the people and the elephant used the same pool, but the pachyderm was taken to the other side of the big pool which housed fish and water snakes. We all enjoyed there too. After his bath, the elephant would put mud all over its body as we applied powder.

Once, this tusker was brought to Ramavilas by its mahout and tied to the Mango tree which used to pelt mangoes. He told us that he would come in the evening to take him back and pulled a few coconut fronds and a few full jackfruits and put them in front of the elephant and went away. He started eating the fronds and then stamped one jackfruit, pulled out the succulent fleshy part with its trunk and put it in its mouth, enjoying it. We admired the strong elephant and the way he stamped the jackfruit and the way he fanned his ears. Suddenly, it started drizzling and the elephant became restless. Soon it started raining cats and dogs and that was the saturation point for the tusker. It started moving, trying to pull the chain, raised its trunk and trumpeted which made us shudder. At length the mahout came, pacified it and slowly unchained it and walked away, to the great relief of all of us.

After all these enjoyments and drama, returning to Palakkad was a very saddening affair. Embracing the pillar tightly, I used to cry loudly and throw tantrums saying that I wouldn't go back to Palakkad, hoping against hope that no one would force me to go back lest the pillar would protect me! My parents had to coax me to change my mind. They would remind me of my friends at Palakkad, Sakuntala and Jayashree who would be terribly missing my company and yearning to see me. My mom had a knack of hitting the nail on the head! That statement was invariably the turning point to change my mind! Then, dressing up and rushing to the gate to catch the bus to the bus stand and then boarding the bus to Palakkad... all would happen in a jiffy. Once I reached my house at Palakkad, I started counting and calculating how many days I had to wait to start our next journey to Cherpulachery.

The scenario changed totally at Palghat; people with a slightly different dialect came and went; my activities and interests changed. From the next day onwards, going to school, studying, playing with friends…….and so on.

"Grandmothers always have time to talk and make you feel special"

- Catherine Pulsifer

CHAPTER-4

Moyan Girls' High School

"We are all travelers in the wilderness of this world, and the best we can find in our travels is an honest friend."

- Robert Louis Stevenson

When I was in 3rd standard, my mother decided that it was time to admit me to Moyan Girls High School. It was her Almamater too. Two or three months after I started going to The Nursery School , my mother had a discussion with one of her ex-teachers, a role model for her and decided to shift me. After a few days, I was told that that teacher would take me with her and admit me in that school. Very reluctantly, I went with my maid to that teacher's house in the morning. She welcomed me and told her son who was sitting there that she was admitting me in her school. To lift my spirits, she also said, "She is a smart girl. She can even speak English." In those days, the schools were mostly Malayalam medium schools, but in that Lions Nursery school English was taught as a subject from the beginning. The teacher's son asked some questions in English like "What's your name and In which class are you studying" etc. and I answered very proudly.

I walked with the teacher to the school and was given a test there. The result was that I was admitted to the fourth standard instead of third, saying that there was no vacancy in the third! Later, my parents insisted that I should continue in fourth standard one more year lest I not complete that required age when I reached tenth standard. I still wonder why my parents did not accompany me to school that day! Another problem was my name. My father wanted it with a particular spelling, but in the school records, it was spelt in a different way. Anyway, I started going to this new school. Sometimes my mother used to accompany me when she went to her tailoring classes. Sometimes, our maid accompanied me.

One Janaki teacher was our class teacher. She used to take all the subjects. She was one of the most excellent teachers I have ever seen. I loved her classes. So many years later, when I became a teacher, I tried some of her teaching techniques in class like dividing the class into two groups and encouraging each group to ask questions and giving them points and announcing the winner group. Another activity was enacting a play or story. We enjoyed all that.

I had new friends. Surprisingly, I didn't miss my old friends. Children have that knack to adapt to new surroundings. We were a group of five or seven girls. There was a peculiar game. We had to think of God and ask Him for some small gifts and it had to be discussed in the group. The next day, somehow, we all got something similar to what we asked for! Or, one of the girls would bring some material similar to that. I was flabbergasted when I got something I asked for. Now I know that it was a trick played by them. Since I was younger than them and also a newcomer, they enjoyed fooling me. That was not all. While playing like Khokho or Catch Me, when we became tired, we stood under a giant tree and thought of God and asked for water. We visualized big glasses of water or juice and consuming that. Surprisingly, it quenched our thirst!

Later, this visualization technique became very handy when I learnt Pranic Healing and Reiki. I learnt that visualization can, to a great extent, help you achieve what you want in life.

The next year, as my parents wanted, I continued in the same class. That year, my friends Sakuntala and Jayashree also joined the same school, but they both were in different sections. Sakuntala's elder sister who was three or four years elder to us also shifted to this school. The school was around one kilometer away from our homes. All of us walked to school together at around 9.30 in the morning, came back home for lunch and again went back to school. The school was from 10 am to 1 pm. Then one hour lunch break and from 2 pm to 4 pm, post lunch sessions. Fridays alone, long lunch break. If I remember correctly, on Fridays lunch break was from 12.30 to 2 pm., to suit the convenience of Muslim students.

Bhurka was not compulsory for Muslim girls. My best friend was one Zubeda. We were together from 5th std to 7th or so. After that she had to shift to Trivandrum since her father was posted there as a judge. Zubeda was a very nice and studious girl. We were in touch for many years. After my wedding, when we shifted to Trivandrum we could meet again, but then slowly, we lost touch. I made a vague attempt to contact her. The only information was that all her three sisters became doctors, but she preferred not to take up that profession. Her brother had acted in a few films, but he passed away at a young age. Another friend of mine was Rosy John. I could not have any contact with her after I left school. At school, for four five years I was appointed as our class leader. In our journey of life, many people travel with us, many board from somewhere and may alight somewhere, some suddenly disappear! No explanation for this phenomenon.

Some classes were thatched sheds. There was a row of these sheds. About five or six months after the school reopened, because of the wear and tear and the mischievous hands of the girls the partitions between the classes got displaced. It was then very difficult to concentrate in class because of the noise from both the sides. Sometimes the partitions were remade and put up.

One day one girl lost her pen and so she complained to the class teacher. The teacher diplomatically asked everyone to search our own bags to see whether by mistake, anyone had kept it inadvertently in her bag. Everyone searched and said that the pen was not in her bag.

The girl who lost the pen wanted the pen back. The teacher was in a dilemma. She went and complained to the Headmistress. In the afternoon, the HM came on rounds. She looked around, scanned everyone with her piercing eyes and asked, "Who took the pen?" Everyone denied. The strict HM went round the class and murmured in the ears of the class teacher and went away.

Then, it was the turn of the class teacher. She said, "The HM had spotted the culprit. She murmured in my ears. Whoever has taken the pen has to return it by tomorrow. Come a little early, leave it at the owner's desk and be calm. If you don't return it, you will be expelled from school." That was that.

The next morning, after everyone assembled in the class, the class teacher asked the girl, "Did you get the pen?"

The girl replied. "Yes, teacher" and raised the pen for all of us to see. Everyone was surprised and relieved too. Then suddenly the teacher let the cat out of the bag. She said triumphantly, "Actually, the HM did not spot the culprit. I went to both the neighboring classes and informed a couple of students what had happened in our class and asked them to come a little early in the morning and notice who is coming early to our class and spot that girl and report to me. They did what I had asked them to do and now we all know the culprit!"

She went on taking class and in between remarked that the culprit was very restless and said that the past was past and asked her not to panic. We all did not know who she was but nobody bothered to find out.

This class teacher was a little short tempered and if we had not done our homework, she used to bang our heads. In those days, there was no problem with such punishments. Now, if any teacher touches a student, he/she is doomed for life. I sometimes feel that punishments, to some extent, are necessary to make a person strong. Our teachers were of various types. There was a music teacher who used to come to class, very shabbily dressed. Up to 5th standard, there were boys and girls in our school. This music teacher, one day very coolly, called a boy and asked him to go to the nearby shop and get one masala dosa for her. The poor boy went and bought and the teacher opened the packet artistically in front of all of us and relished the dosa, licking her fingers. Half her class would go like this. This practice was repeated for many days. I wonder how she escaped the prying eyes of the strict HM who had eyes all over her head!

I had a few friends in my class. I was in the habit of bringing a few of my friends home one by one on Fridays during lunch break. On Fridays, we had an extra half an hour for lunch. One day before that, I had to tell my mom. A friend of mine, Valsala, was very much interested in coming home with me for lunch. We both walked together slowly, had lunch. She relished my mom's food and after that we went back. That evening, she had epilepsy and she blacked out. Most of us were seeing someone having fits for the first time and so we got scared. Immediately, our class teacher came near her and took care of her. It lasted only for a few seconds. By then the bell rang. Her aunt was a teacher there. Valsala went home with her aunt. A few days later, when we went to school, we got very sad news. Valsala had gone to take a bath in the tank and there she got fits and got drowned! We were shocked. I was all the more shocked because she came to my house one day to have lunch and we were sitting on the same bench and we both had the same name. The HM and some teachers went to her house for condolence.

The HM was a very efficient lady. She was my mother's teacher too. In Kerala, strikes and protests are very common. The condition was the same then too. Once, the students of all the schools were called for a strike by the opposition party. Educational institutions, except our school and shops were all closed down. The HM didn't budge to the demands. Then, from the boys' school nearby, students came and sternly asked her to close down the school. She hesitated, but the ferocious boys said, "Close down your institution, lady, otherwise we'll chop off your head." She fell before this threat and was subdued and immediately the boys started ringing the long bell. Ringgggggg……

The next day, again we all went to school without problem. We couldn't do away with problems all together. The next challenge cropped up in another field.

Suddenly, in Palghat, there was an infestation of snails. The story says that someone had brought a couple of snails from Sri Lanka to do some experiments. This person's father was sick and eventually, the old man passed away. By then the snails had multiplied and this gentleman gave instructions to the servant to dig a pit, put salt in that and put the snails and again throw salt on those and close the pit so that those could be wiped out, otherwise these would play havoc. The obedient servant dug the pit, put the snails in that and might have sprinkled some salt on top and closed the pit. Some escaped and they spread all over the place and started consuming leaves and plants. People could not grow anything properly. It became a big menace.

Apart from destroying plants, they became harmful for people also. Some discharge from the snail caused blisters in the body of humans when they accidentally came into contact with each other. In those days chappals were not compulsory. Some wore, some preferred not to wear. At Nursery school it was compulsory to wear shoes with a uniform. But at the other school it was not compulsory. To cut the long story short, I developed a blister between my toes and my mother tried wrapping a cloth dipped in salt water, but it didn't help much. It was difficult for me to walk and at last Dr. Kesavan Nair, our family doctor was consulted and he suggested that it should be poked with a sterilized pin and some ointment applied. He thought that my father would do that at home since I was not taken to the doctor. Moreover, my father had studied at the medical college for two years and then he dropped out feeling that that was not his cup of tea. So my father did what the doctor asked him to do and slowly but surely, I recovered.

Now, before that, since I could walk very slowly, the other girls coming with me to school started mumbling and started walking fast, leaving me to limp to school. I felt very sad and told my mom about it. I couldn't blame them, so at my own pace, I inched my way to school. Again I started disliking school.

Moreover, one day, I was walking at my own pace to school and I met someone who looked like Lord Muruga. He was walking with his vel in hand. The very form scared and puzzled me! Wondering whether it was real Muruga, I wanted to turn back and run, but I could not. Somehow, I reached school. The next day also, a similar experience. This time, it was not Muruga, but Krishna. The next day. I refused to go to school and explained everything to mom. I complained that the other girls were not waiting for me. And I had to limp alone and I had to face different 'Gods' on the way, all alone! She felt pity on me and consoled me by saying that it must be someone disguised as the Gods to fool people and collect money. But she made our maid accompany me to school. Coming back was not much of a problem because many students walked together on the road. Within a few days, I became all right and started going with my friends to and from school.

Anyway, I learnt one more lesson in life- help yourself. Self-help is the best help. You can't expect someone or the other to always help you. Each one has his/her own problems. Overburdening them with our problems is not right. After a few days, I recovered completely.

The walk and talk and laughter together continued. In the evenings I went to Sakuntala's or Jayashree's house to play with the girls over there. I was the only girl in my house, so they all rarely came to my house to play with me. It was easier for me to go to their houses. They all came to my house once in a way, to see our pretty garden which my parents maintained beautifully. It was full of flowers of different types and colours, some with fragrance, visited by butterflies with different patterns on their wings. It was a feast for the eyes.

There was another attraction in our house-the doggie Princy and the cat blacky and its kittens. I shall talk about them later.

Sakuntala's house was diagonally opposite to mine. They all used to sleep in the main bedroom upstairs. By 8.30 pm, the children used to go to the bedroom. In our house, we all used to sit in our sit out, after our dinner. Our sit out was covered with a designed grill so none could enter without opening the front door. However, we could see Sakuntala's bedroom very clearly and we could converse. There was a small window opening to our house in their bedroom. Sakuntala's younger sister Nalini used to sit on the window sill and start a conversation," Valsala, did you have your dinner?" I would answer that question and ask her a counter question. The conversation would last only for a few minutes. By then, the horn of their father's car could be heard. Immediately, they would scream together, " father….." and switch off the light and lay down. After that , no sound could be heard. In our house, we would have a hearty laugh and we would continue with our prate.

"Best friends don't expect anything from you. They just accept you the way you are."

- Maxime Lagace

CHAPTER-5

MY Brother

"Once a brother, always a brother, no matter the distance, no matter the difference and no matter the issue."

- Byron Pulsifer

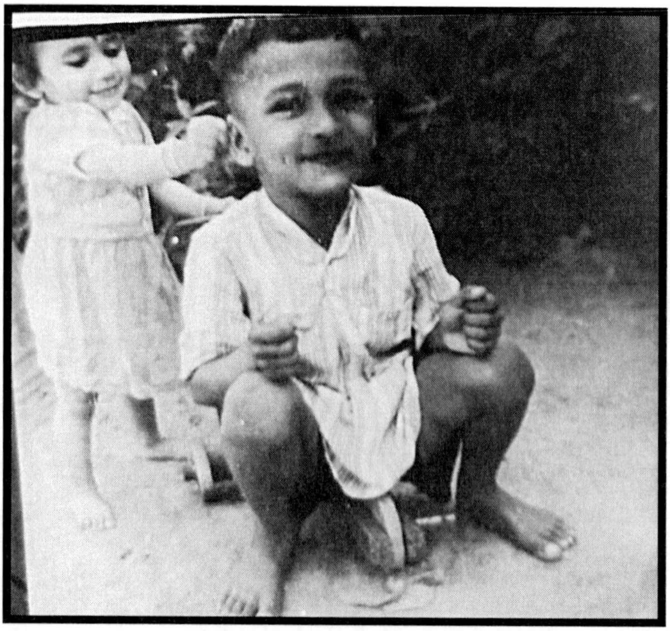

At this juncture, I should say that my brother had a hand in instilling fear in me. He told me that we should be good children and never tell a lie or hurt others. Otherwise, God would punish us by cutting us into pieces and frying our flesh in burning oil. He also told me to check every night whether I had told a lie that day or done something wrong. One day, thinking about all these, I couldn't sleep and was tossing my head and blinking when my mom caught me and asked me what I was up to. Very reluctantly, I blurted out everything, on the verge of crying. She consoled me saying that that was not true and reprimanded my brother for scaring me like that!

Later I realized that he said all these with the intention of making me an honest person like my father. I should say that he had a big role in teaching me many things like chess, table tennis and a few card games since all these could be played indoors. For cricket alone he didn't call me, for that was then considered as a game exclusively for boys. Moreover, he had friends to play with and if they were short of a player, my mother did not mind joining (batting alone, not running). They played with an ordinary ball and bat and stumps made of different parts of the coconut tree!

We had a long dining table on which we both, my brother and myself played table tennis. Chess was a later introduction. Our bachelor uncle was an excellent chess player who used to play postal chess even with international chess players. From here, he would make a move, record it on a postcard and send it to his opponent. From there, the opponent would record his move and send him. If I remember correctly, he was once an international champion in correspondence Chess. This uncle, Kuttiettan, as we addressed him, got a lot of coloured cards from these foreign players whenever he won and all those cards were given to my brother and me. We divided these cards equally between us and then played chess and the loser had to give the winner one card from the lot as a prize. Most of the time, my brother won even though I too had won. We both used to sit for hours together and played this marvellous game when everyone else slept till our mother came and reprimanded us! But it was real fun.

We didn't know the different opening games and end games, but were thorough with the rules and also the moves, castling and the intricacies. In those days, chess was not very popular and there were no competitions in schools or colleges, so we didn't get into the nuances of various moves. Now, the scenario is different. There are chess tournaments everywhere and chess classes are aplenty. Only after becoming a teacher did I get a chance to play chess and win tournaments! My uncle's chess books I had, but one prize book was borrowed from me by someone but never returned!

My brother also could take part in chess tournaments only after taking up a job. He was, however, a cricket player and a tennis player too in college. Immediately after his graduation in Physics from the Victoria college, he got a job at The NSS college, Ottappalam. He used to go to that college from home. For a few days he was staying at a hostel at Ottappalam.

He had certain idiosyncrasies. When I was learning classical music, my brother made fun of me by showing faces, for he couldn't enjoy this type of music, but he loved film songs, especially, Hindi and English. However, he couldn't sing. Listening to Hindi songs when he had holidays was a regular pastime for him. The best part was, giving marks for each song, for which, Mukesh always got the first mark. He was an ardent fan of Mukesh to whom he had sent a few letters and his replies Ettan still stores. My favourite singers were Talat Mehmood and Lata Mangeshkar.

Ettan liked going for Movies too. Cricket was another passion of his. My father helped him make an album with brown paper, cut and stitched and made a book and he cut and pasted the pictures of great cricket players batting and bowling in various styles. In those days LIFE magazines were available which had pictures of cricket players and cinema stars. My brother had a good collection of these. Since my father helped him make an album, I too wanted one to stick some ad pictures, for then I knew nothing about cricket. I told my wish to my dad and he immediately gathered some leftover brown papers, cut them, stitched them and made a book and gave it to me. I looked at my brother's album and then mine. His was very neat and tidy whereas mine was like a crumpled garment! I was so disappointed, but since my father gave that, I kept quiet.

Ettan even had a couple of stamp albums and small photo albums. Whatever he had, I too wanted. My father made sure that I too got one. Once both of us were sitting in a room, I on the cot and he, on the floor with his stamp album and a glass of water to stick the stamps, humming a tune. I was observing him, shaking my legs silently when suddenly, unexpectedly, my feet touched the glass and the water spilled on the album, drenching it! My brother started howling and wailing, pointing his finger at me and blaming blatantly that I did it purposely. I tried to say that it was accidental, but he wouldn't listen. Suddenly, I sensed someone standing at the door assessing the scene. Unfortunately, it wasn't my father, but uncle Kuttyettan. He was so angry that he gave me one slap and I started crying pleading my innocence. I couldn't control my sorrow and fear and I started passing urine. He said I had to behave properly and warned me not to repeat it and went away and my parents came and consoled me. They told Ettan not to make so much fuss over a silly thing. He retorted, "Silly thing? It may be silly for you, but for me, it is my prized possession." Wiping his eyes with the edge of his sleeves, he went away, taking his treasure leaving me gaping and regretting my carelessness! After some time, I overcame my grief.

I remembered that I too had some prized possessions- a few playing cards, one from a different pack of cards which my closest friend Zubada gave me and some matchbox pictures, a few round pebbles which we girls used to play with! My fussy brother didn't have any of these! That thought made me smile.

Ettan liked to do some experiments. There were a bunch of small slides of coloured pictures in our house. It must be one of our ancestor's. My brother used to occupy one bedroom upstairs. He used to use torch light, prism etc. darken the room and project the pictures on the wall. The pictures would be zoomed and those looked like film pictures. The only difference was that those were not motion pictures. Those were stills. I used to look at the images, wonderstruck and with a lot of admiration for my brother.

Another thing about him was that he used to keep his books neatly stacked on his shelf, but my books, by the end of the year, would be like a pack of displaced pappadams.

Even when he was working at NSS college, Ottappalam, Ettan played cricket and even took the team to other colleges to play. When he was working at Ottapalam, our PM was Lal Bahadur Shastri. He persuaded people to 'miss a meal'. Ettan wanted to show that he was an ardent fan of the PM and, I think, every Friday, used to tell mom not to keep dinner for him. Mom was very happy that he was turning out to be a good, sacrificing human being and when we were having dinner, she would look at him with admiration. After a few days, somehow, the cat was out of the bag. His agenda was to visit the Indian coffee House every Friday, while returning from Ottapalam and fill his stomach with the mouthwatering mutton cutlets, sumptuous samosa, cold coffee and the like! Knowing this, I became green with envy.

Anyway, he didn't work there for long. Our uncle who was in the army called him to the place where he was posted and helped him get a job. That was yet another lesson. At times of utter necessity, someone will come as God and help us .

My brother was first posted at Agra, but later, he shifted to Kanpur. I still remember his coming to Palakkad on leave. Dad and myself went to the station to receive him the first time he came down. Since the wait was a bit long and it was getting a little late, we three stepped into the restaurant at the station to have a light refreshment. That was the first time we ate at the restaurant at the station. We found the bread-butter-jam very delicious. He had brought sarees for me and mom and also various other things for all the family members.

The next year also, I remember going to the station with dad to receive Ettan. The train was late. At last, it came, spreading the black smoke. There was a screech and a sound like someone sighing and the train halted. I liked to listen to the different sounds at the railway station. The vendors started moving, calling out, "chai..chai", "vada,

vada, vada", "biryani…biryaniyey" in their own tones. Paper wallas, plantain sellers, people who got down from the train, travellers who got down to collect water (there was no bottled water in those days), those who came just to see the trains…all these people walked through the platform, some sauntered and others sprinted, nearly dashing against others. Some were walking as if in a dream! My dad walked up and down, looking for my brother, but no brother. We were terribly disappointed for we didn't know what had happened. It was not very easy to contact anybody since there were no cell phones, and no land lines in most of the houses.

The whistling of the engine startled me. My father was in a pensive mood, but tried to camouflage it cautiously when someone walked towards us. On coming closer, we recognised him as my cousin, Kuttykrishna Ettan who was returning after his Ranji Trophy match. Dad explained to him everything and my cousin remarked that he might have missed the train and told us not to worry. Disappointed, we went back. Convincing my mom was a Herculean task. Somehow, we spent the day and the next morning, again dad went to the station. That day my brother was there and he explained how he missed the train. Since he arrived safely, no one bothered about the reason for his not reaching the previous day.

When I think of my brother, I remember an incident. After he took up a job at Kanpur, he used to come every year on leave. Our favourite eatery was the Coffee House. We visited the Coffee House mainly for eating the mutton cutlets which were yummy. The servers wearing special uniforms and their friendly ways always amused us. I was happy that I too could go to the Coffee House which my brother visited when he 'missed a meal'.

Another favourite place of ours was Malampuzha. We four once went to the Malampuzha gardens. We enjoyed roaming around there, saw the giant sculpture of the Medusa, visited the Japanese gardens, went through the ropeway and tiredly came down to board the bus to go home. I didn't forget to go round the garden in the toy train. We went to the zoo too.

It was getting late. The full moon started peeping through the clouds, the pinkish evening sky was changing its colour. Two buses went away carrying maximum passengers. The next one came. Somehow my mother and I could board the crowded bus. My mother started panicking and called out to my dad asking whether he was there and he answered that he was very much there, but his dhoti had gone! There was a roar of laughter. Then with the help of someone he could gather his dhoti, wear it and board the bus. Again my mom started saying that her son Ramkumar alone couldn't board and requested the conductor to allow him to board. The conductor, feeling pity for my mother, called out," Is there any Ramkumar there? Your mom wants you to board" and asked the others to give way to him. Immediately, half a dozen people called out. "I am Ramkumar. Let me get in." The conductor was in a dilemma. At last, the actual Ramkumar pushed and pulled and squirmed through the crowd claiming that he was the actual Ramkumar and got into the bus and it moved forward leaving the impostors behind.

"A brother is a friend who walks with you on the journeys of life, making it more memorable."

- Unknown

Malampuzha

CHAPTER-6

Father's absence

"A dad is the anchor upon which his children stand."

My father, as I have already mentioned, had studied two years at the Kilpauk Medical College, but then he quit. After a few years he took up a job at the Ordnance factory at Jabalpur. After marriage, my mother accompanied him to Jabalpur. Unfortunately, after a couple of years he had to quit since there was retrenchment. Coming back to Kerala, he started a Dairy Farm at Palakkad, but that was also not a success. He had to wind up. Now, when I was in 5th or 6th standard, he got an offer to work on the border roads in Bhutan. We all were very sad when he left for Bhutan and I felt very lonely.

I was learning classical music under one Krishnan Namboodiri who was a student at the Chembai Music Academy. He was basically from a family of Poojaris. He was the only one in his family who was interested in classical music and came to Palakkad to pursue his coaching in music. His father thought that he was crazy. He was doing pooja at the temple attached to a Tharavadu in Palakkad and staying there and at the same time, attending classes at the Music Academy.

This music master used to come home every day except Sunday to teach me music. His music academy and my school were close to each other. The timings were also more or less the same. This gentleman was very tall and sometimes he used to reach my house before I did. I started making a fuss because I wanted to relax and have some snacks after coming back from school.

I am mentioning my music master here because when he knew that my dad was going to Bhutan, he conveyed the news that from that house also someone was going to Bhutan. At the station we met him and both, my father and that gentleman travelled together and worked together in Bhutan. We all were relieved that another man from Palakkad was with my father.

His taking up a job in Bhutan happened when Ettan and I were students. I think I was in 5th std then. The misery of someone you love and respect going away from you is unbearable!

We got letters from dad regularly. He thoughtfully wrote to all the three of us separately so that none of us would feel neglected. Sometimes mother requested the music master to post our letters to dad on his way back. My music master was a six footer, lean and fair, with a vermilion adorning his forehead. He was a good singer with a powerful voice. Master never used to take part in any music competition at the academy because he felt that he was older than all his classmates. He deemed it not right to take part in competitions with them. He was very good at theory also. Sometimes my mom and this master had lively discussions about Carnatic music.

Life had to go on and I started looking forward to going to Cherpulassery. My granny(mother's mother), who used to go and stay with my uncles came back and started staying with us since Father had gone to Bhutan. I didn't want to forgo my trip to Cherpulchery. My mother too didn't want to deny me that! The net result was that my uncle, Kuttiettan, started taking me to Cherpulcheri. My brother is five years older than me, so he wanted to go alone, not with me and Kuttiettan. Along with Kuttiettan, I walked to the bus stand opposite to the railway station from where the smell of coal which I liked came. This time, no horse cart, but something more attractive happened. There was one Lakshmi Vilas Hotel near the bus stand. Kuttyettan took me there and treated me with lip smacking Poori-masala, Jilebi and coffee which I used to relish. At Kongad, there was a halt for about fifteen minutes for the driver and conductor to have their breakfast to boost their energy.

Around 9 am. We were at Cherpulassery. The whole family with my granny, aunty, uncle and their children would be there, all smiles, in the front verandah. After a few minutes, we, cousins, would disappear in the sprawling field which was surrounded by walls. Kuttieattan would have light refreshments with the other members, rest for some time, talk with the family members and after having lunch, went back to Palakkad. Before going back, he would call me and bid me farewell.

For Onam, we all got small dhoti (paavumundu) from our paternal granny at Cherpulachery. It was the short holiday after Onam, and my cousin Devi waited for my arrival to get the dhoti from granny (achamma). The Onam flower carpet was special and placing of 'matheru' and I think, on the last day, Vamana {all, with clay} with a palm leaf umbrella. I don't remember who did the flower carpet everyday. Devi & I were not involved in that. Our main attraction was the small hut made by Ramanesan. It was a small hut made with sticks, bamboo, coconut leaves and ropes. In the morning, half the time we both spent there with our toy vessels 'making' rice and curry and the rest with stones, leaves and water! Then we wandered around the compound, climbed trees. We had a favourite mango tree on which both of us could sit comfortably. Devi was a very kind and innocent girl. One day we both were having pastries when Ramanesan came that way. Devi immediately took a big piece from her share and gave it to him, murmuring to me in a hushed tone," Poor thing! I don't know when he tasted one!" and the excited Ramanesan relished it, saying it was very tasty.

When we grew up we found it very interesting to play 56. It's a card game. Even adults played with much enthusiasm. It could be played with 6 or 8 members. With 4 people 28 could be played. It's not as interesting as 56.

During summer holidays, the fun was more. That is the period of mangoes, jackfruits, cashew fruits and in some years, blueberry and jambakka. There were varieties of mangoes and jackfruits. In the evening, the ladies of the house and the helpers sat around the cut jackfruit and segregated the edible part and the seeds. While doing this each one helped himself/herself with a few pieces. It's entertaining to even watch them do this. Mostly, one evening, jackfruit and the next evening, different types of mangoes. If there were not enough people to help with the jackfruit work, it would be cut into different portions called "ori" and given to each one who had to clean and separate the fleshy part and eat. The seeds were collected and later, cleaned, removing the coatings and cut into pieces to prepare different types of dishes. One should eat these dishes sparingly for it may produce gas in the stomach. The leftover parts were given to the cow called "kali Payyu." She used to relish that. She was of a peculiar colour-blackish brown on her upper part and a little light brown on her legs. She was well fed with large udders that supplied a large quantity of milk. The ghee made with the milk she gave tasted very nice.

We children loved to see Vishukani in the summer holidays. When I went to Ramavilas during summer holidays, I carried the crackers and sparklers Kuttiettan had bought for us and handed it over to achamma. They also used to buy a lot of crackers, flower pots, Vishnu's wheel, kambithiri, pookutty etc. Two three days before Vishu, achamma kept the whole thing in the sun for some time to dry. The previous day of Vishu it would be divided among all of us. Early in the morning granny would call one by one to see the Kani. Radhikedathy would make a special appeal that she should be called first and shown the Kani. Then we would get kaineettam from the elders.

During Vishu time, a particular group of birds we call Vishu Pakshis appeared and chirped. We, children made a parody of their chirping:

"Vithum Kaikkottum, Kallan chkkayituu.
Kandal mindanda, kondoy thinnotte."

Meaning, a thief came and plucked a jackfruit, but don't bother, let him go and eat it.

It is surprising that we hear only one bird chirp like this at a time. No chorus chirping!

At the start of the Monsoon you would find many changes in nature. You could hear thunder, the temperature would come down, and at the first drizzle, you would find insects like "flying termites." These are very disturbing and sometimes fall into the cooked food also! Whenever these appeared at Cherpalchery, Ramanesan would collect a bunch of palm leaves and burn them. Seeing the light, they would go near that and get burnt! It was sad to watch them burn to death!.

Once, when I was there at Cherpulachery, I developed a fever. My aunt gave Maliniedathy the responsibility to take care of me. She made Horlicks for me and the cherubic figure sat by me side, inquiring how I was. I relished the Horlicks , for I was tasting it for the first time. At Palghat, my mom used to add Bournvita to milk and made me drink which I disliked to the core. I didn't like milk at all. Moreover, if the cream of that milk went into the mouth, I would vomit. The

Horlicks given to me by my cousin, I liked. Malinieadathy's innocent face with small brown eyes and her concern for me enchanted me. She was a very fair, beautiful girl whose thick hair flowed down her knees. I used to admire that.

Maliniedathy had a small notebook in which she used to write down each day's news headlines. She was a very calm person who did not show any hurry in doing anything, let it be eating the titbits given to her or wearing the new dress purchased for her. Her younger sister, Radhikedathy was slightly different from this. She was more aesthetically inclined. She has thick, straight hair and a beautiful voice. During Ramayana month, after growing up, she enjoyed reading Ramayanam loudly in the night which achamma encouraged. Rdhikedathy was fond of eating goodies.

Once, she opened the door of a cupboard where different items were stored. There she found a small bottle with something like broken pieces of laddu. She thought that Maliniedathy had preserved her share of laddu, in that broken form with the intention of taking it later ,and took a handful of that and put it into her mouth. Getting the frothy taste, she spat out the brackish substance and tried to complain to her mother about the horrible tasting laddu powder! An exasperated grunt from her made my aunty look into the matter and on investigation she found that the so called laddu powder was actually Lux flakes which was available in those days to wash soft, silk sarees.

Radhikedathy was emotional too. She was good at reading stories out loud from different magazines to everyone. I remember, one day, her reading out a touching story while we were (only girls) sitting under the jackfruit tree near the big car shed. Her emotional reading moved us into tears. Once, the cook was preparing chicken curry. Normally we saw it only on the table, but that day, while loitering through the backyard we found the cook killing the chickens and cleaning them. Radhikedathy refused to consume that chicken curry. Aachamma's chicken curry was very delicious. I wonder when she got rid of the aversion towards chicken! Cherpulchery trip, as always, came to an end within a few days.

During my father's absence, two weddings took place in our family. One was the wedding of my Uncle Appammama's daughter and another was my uncle Unnimama's. Pappedathy's wedding was at Ottapalam and that of Unnimama's was at Bangalore. For Pappedathy's wedding, Appammama gave all of us new dresses and clothes. My cousin Radhikedathy and myself were assigned the task of carrying the 'talam' to welcome the bridegroom. It was not so elaborate and showy in those days. Anyway, many invitees were there and some European ladies too. My brother was given the task of talking to them in English and explaining everything because it was a new experience for them. That uncle was the conservator of forest at that time.

The unusual thing about that wedding was that cashew nuts and lime juice were served in between breakfast and lunch. One old uncle was sitting there along with the guests and since this was a new introduction, he was thrilled and called the server again and again to grab a handful of nuts, not bothered about the hawk-like eyes of the other guests. If the server did not notice his bidding hands, he didn't mind clapping his hands to attract his attention. People started murmuring and gossipping at this. The wedding ceremony was a simple affair in Kerala in those days. Not much pomp and show and 'save the date' and drones and all that. While having lunch the guests were entertained by a music concert.

A few days after Pappedathy's wedding , uncle asked my mother whether she would allow him and aunty to take care of me by taking me with them, but my mother refused.

Unnimama's wedding was in Bangalore one week after this wedding. My mom and brother, myself and Mohanettan (ppammama's son) boarded the train. In those days no A/C compartments. It was an ordinary, 2nd class compartment. Mohanettan managed to occupy the upper berth. He spread his bedding. All the four of us were sitting on one side. That meant that one could sleep there. Two of us should sleep down, spreading our bedding. The next morning, we reached Bangalore and my uncle had come to take us. We missed my father then. He was the pillar of our strength. We went to our relative's house. The wedding went off very well and the bride & groom were brought to our relative's house the next day. There was a small party there and then, again, another party at some hall in the evening hosted by my aunt's dad.

After a couple of days we returned. My uncle and aunt came down to our house at Palakkad only after both of them could take leave for enough days. My aunt was working at the Income Tax office. My granny was very happy to meet her youngest son and wife. Since she couldn't travel to Bangalore, she didn't attend the wedding. Later, when my uncle, Kochammama got transferred to Bangalore, my granny was able to go and stay with him and she could meet Unnimama and family also.

Unnimama and family came every two years or so. They had three children, one girl and two boys. These children were very much younger than me, so I had a special affection for them. When they went out for a walk, sometimes , they took me too.

Uncles and families came and stayed and went back. Our life at Lakshmi Vilas went on. For a few days after they all went, I felt miserable, but then time would take care of everything. One year after dad had gone to Bhutan, we all eagerly waited for him to come on leave. He worked in Bhutan for four or five years. Whenever he came, he brought a lot of things for us at Palghat and also to those at Ramavilas. After one month, after he returned we all felt very sad. He too missed us and at last decided to quit and come back.

As the seasons changed the atmosphere and activities also changed. At one season the whole of Palakkad experienced severe winds, winds passing through the Palghat gap chapped our skins.

At different seasons, seasonal vegetables were brought for sale by single vendors. I loved the thuvara season because I loved that vegetable. Moreover, a woman with an enchanting smile brought that. She had a gold chain around her neck with many small pendants. Every year she added one pendant to it.

Another season the houses were whitewashed and painted.

One season there was Kodungallor Bharani. Our maid servant was an oracle too. She was an ardent devotee of Kodungallor Amma. She adorned the oracle's costume, prayed at the small temple attached to her own house, got possessed and walked away to different houses and prophesied. From all those houses she got cash and different things. After a few days, she would go to Kodungallur with her people and other oracles.

Chinna was an expert in relieving people from others' evil eyes! Sometimes mother would say, "Chinna, this girl is very lethargic now-a-days. Why don't you do something to save her from the evil eyes? After finishing all her work, Chinna would ask me to sit on the bench and take some sacred ash, chant something inaudible. It went on for at least thirty minutes. In between, she would start yawning. At times, the yawns became too long. Her mouth would remain wide open with her stained teeth visible and I sometimes wondered whether she would swallow me up! Or was she swallowing the effects of the evil eyes? As a young child I could never believe when she said many people had cast their evil eye on me, but now, as I am a healer, I wonder whether it could have been correct. After completing her feat successfully, she would leave satisfied that she could save me from the evil eyes of many. Mom used to give money for her 'services'.

At different seasons people celebrated different functions. There was a cousin of my father, Balammama, who was slightly different from others. He was a bachelor who was not very educated. His main hobby was visiting different relatives of his every now and then. Since there were many relatives, he didn't have a problem spending one day with one family. He was sure to come to our house at the time of the Kalpathy car festival. His routine was the following. By evening he would turn up, walk around talking to the people in the house. He would vomit all the news gathered from different quarters without looking into the faces of people. He imparted only the correct news, or rather, the news he got. He was not imaginative enough to add colour to the information. In a sing-song tone, and with a nasal sound, without looking at anybody's face, he conveyed the messages. He relished food and didn't criticize anybody and anything. After dinner, he would retire to his sleeping area. Very early in the morning, we could see him walk away, only to come back after sometime. He preferred to go to a nearby river to take a bath. Balammama would be there, right on time for breakfast. After breakfast, he would take his cloth bag and long grandfather umbrella with a curved handle and walk away without telling anybody anything! He wouldn't come back to the same house. Next, he would go to another house.

Once, Balammama turned up out of season, unexpectedly. All of us wondered what was happening in Palakkad. He said, "Tomorrow they are inaugurating the distribution of Malampuzha water in Palakkad. I've come to witness that." In his pure Malayalam, Balammama said, "Sudda jala vitarana paddhathi." He would get all the news of the district and present himself wherever possible. He was a person of equanimous mind and wouldn't become overjoyed or disappointed. He could accept anything! It's very difficult to find people like him.

Nobody minded Balammama's arrival because he was a very gentle man who didn't have any intention of hurting or overburdening anyone. He was taken care of by his sister or someone. He was such a simple man that he didn't need an invitation to attend a wedding or a funeral. He was welcome everywhere. At Cherpulachery, the bus conductors also knew him and sometimes they didn't even collect ticket fare from him. His only predicament was that he used to get brief convulsions. Since it didn't last for long, he didn't encounter serious problems. However, he ran into some unexpected issues.

Once, he went to Ernakulam to his relative's place. He went there to attend a wedding. He stayed at another relative's house. At night, one family member fell sick and she needed medicine. There was no male member to go, so Balammama was requested to go to get medicine. With a chit, and money, he went out and got the medicine from some nearby pharmacy, but since he was not sure of the way back and darkness started setting in, he had to loiter around, trying to find an area he was familiar with.

The inspector of a speeding police van, patrolling that area saw him, backed the van and stopped near him. The suspicious police inspector eyed him dramatically and questioned him, twitching his mustache. Somehow, he managed to say he came out to get medicine for his relative. The inspector had his own doubts and ushered him into the van. It was difficult for them to elicit an answer from him. The lady who sent him to get the medicine panicked since he didn't return. Her sickness must have doubled. At last , they got information that he was taken away by the police. Waiting for him and worried, she and her daughter might have fallen into a slumber. By then, it was morning and the man of the house returned and understanding the graveness of the situation, he rushed to the police station and explained to them and brought him back. At home they asked him why he boarded the van. He could have shown the paper which had their address. Then he said, "It was okay. They didn't hurt me. Moreover, there were some ladies also in the van." Poor man. He didn't know that the "ladies" were the call girls, rounded up by the police from various spots.

Anyway the lucky Balammama was rescued, unscathed from the police station and he didn't have to miss the wedding. For the wedding, many people from Cherpulchery had come. The wedding was to take place at a hall on the 3rd or 4th floor of a building. People were going up to the hall. For some people who had come from Cherpulchery, going by lift was a new experience. A bunch of them got into the lift from the ground floor. Anandavaliamma was going by a lift for the first time. She huddled at a corner of the lift. It went up. Everyone except our 'heroine' got out of the lift and carrying a set of people from that floor the lift went to the ground floor. Everyone got out except Anandavaliamma. Again a few others boarded and the lift went up. Anandavaliamma didn't know what to do and scratched her head thinking what to do when her cousin got in and this time when they reached the third floor, she led her out of the lift!

I think Balammama returned to his house safely along with the others.

CHAPTER-7

My Maternal Grandparents and Uncles and their Families

"I couldn't imagine what it would be like to be one of so many, to have not just parents and siblings but cousins and aunts and uncles, an entire tribe to claim as your own. Maybe you would feel lost in the crowd. Or sheltered by it. Whatever the case, one thing was for sure: like it or not, you'd never be alone."

\- Sarah Dessen

"Some of the most important conversations I've ever had occurred at my family's dinner table."

\- BOB EHRLICH

My grandfather

My grandmother

My maternal house

My mother's family

This was true in my case. I had a loving family with not only my parents and brother, but grandmothers, uncles and aunts and first cousins and distant cousins. Ofcourse, all of us were not living together. We met sometimes. When there are so many people in the family, a lot of interactions and counseling happens. Now-a-days, that is not the case. Most of the families are nuclear families and there is a lot of hush-hush about everything! Something is missing there!

Unnimama and Ammayi came to Palakkad every year and Ammayi made sure that she brought nice dress materials for me and also sweets to the family and also to Appamama's family after they settled down at Palakkad. Later, when I started wearing sarees, she started bringing sarees. They had three children, one girl, Premlatha and two boys, Prem Anand and Prem Mohan. All the three were very cute and I used to look forward to their arrival.

They used to go for a walk in the evening and after coming back, Lata used to lisp to me, "Valsaledathy, we had kalla pappu vada (Kadala parippu vada) today when we went for a walk. One day, Unnimama was saying, "Today, when we went out, Lata saw a small girl wearing a dress, one sleeve had a hole in it. Lata , giggling, went near her and putting her finger into the hole, started tickling her, saying, "kichu kichu kichu….." and the frightened girl started wailing! She used to put two of her fingers upside down, into her mouth and suck. Premanand was so cute with big smiling eyes and he used to come behind me asking me to give him a bath. Once when they all came, Prem already had recovered from a fracture in his leg. Muttikulangara is a place in Palakkad where some medicated oil is made, especially for those who had a fracture. Unnimama went there and bought some oil and it was applied on Prem's leg. After some days he was able to walk properly, but if any one mentioned that, he would become so conscious that he would start walking with a slight limp to the amusement of all of us.

The coming of Kochchammama and family and Unnimama and family made all of us very happy. But they never landed together. Each family came at different times, maybe not to burden my mother who had to do all the work. We had, ofcourse, a maid to do the top work. Kochammama narrated military stories and entertained us and Unnimama entertained us with his stories of magic and how he started performing on stage. He was a good photographer too.

Once, when Kochammama was posted on the border, he decided to put Rammohan, his son, at the boarding school at Ooty- Lovedale. I remember going to Ooty along with my uncle and family and my mom. I shivered since I was going to a cold place for the first time. Actually, my uncle asked my mom whether she would like to put me there, but my mom refused. Uncle got transferred to Bangalore later only and then Ramu was taken away from Ooty. There Kichu, the younger brother of Ramu was born. There was a gap of around ten years between them.

Appammama was actually my mother's first cousin. His mom passed away when he was a baby and my granny (mother's mother) only took care of him. His father, later, married my father's mother and so he was my father's step brother too. He married my father's first cousin. We have gone and stayed with that uncle's family at different places like Coimbatore, Calicut etc. He was very fond of all of us. Once, when my brother developed some skin problem and was suffering. He became very upset and immediately took all the four of us to his house at Coimbatore and took him to a renowned skin specialist and comforted him and mom. Ettan became all right within about 10 days. I still remember the smell of that brown ointment given to him by the doctor. I, as a small child didn't realize the seriousness of the problem, but was extremely happy to bunk school! This uncle retired as the conservator of forests. When we went to stay with him, he took us to see elephants-tamed elephants which were given his nieces' and nephews' names. It was fun to go near them and touch them and feed them.

My granny (ammamma) was able to stay with his family also. His wife was a very beautiful lady. A couple of years after their daughter's wedding, uncle retired and settled down at Palakkad. Their daughter was also at Palakkad since her husband was a professor at The Victoria College.

Appammama was the first one to bring a kerosene stove to our house. Until then, only the old type of stove where you burn wood was available. Lighting that and also cleaning the vessels used were difficult tasks. Mom was very happy to try that kerosene stove, but she didn't do away with the ordinary, traditional stove. We got enough dried palm leaves and wood pieces and broken branches. My mom was very careful with spending money. She never spent money unnecessarily. She was very intelligent and was able to manage things efficiently. In those days many girls did not have good education, but she was allowed to complete her Matriculation at Victoria College. Even though she wanted to do medicine, she was not allowed to since she should go to Madras to study medicine. Her people were not for it. She couldn't do BS.c also since her subject was not offered at Victoria.

My mother was a good singer and violinist. She was a badminton player too.

In those days, ladies had a lot of work at home. She made it a point to make me also share the work. So, I was able to sweep and swab and drag water from the well in the absence of a maid. I even liked deshelling coconuts and cleaning fish. Cleaning vessels and washing clothes, I did not like. However, my brother was not made to do any work. In those days, gents normally didn't do any such work. But my father was an exception. He used to help my mom in cooking and cutting vegetables.

We rarely went to Elppulli, to our ancestral home. We went there in the morning and returned in the evening by bus. While going to Elappulli, there used to be a severe breeze since the bus was going in the eastern direction. Mom used to cover her nose with umbrella cloth since she used to feel suffocated. Wherever they went, my parents used to take umbrellas with them and also very big kerchiefs. Those kerchiefs were multipurpose kerchiefs. I loved such short trips. Mom's cousins were there and their children were there to play with me. Mom had pleasant memories about Elappulli and her holidays there as a girl. Our family deity is Meenkulathil Bhagavathy, at Pallassana, but since my dad and mom were not pious, we had never gone there in those days. The people over there used to keep Devi's kumkum very carefully, for they all believed that Devi would protect her ardent devotees. In those days, I didn't know what to believe, but now, I am certain that Devi would help and protect her devotees.

People over there are famous for making different snacks like Murukku, Porulankaya, kesari, Sukhiyan and the like. Ladies over there are very famous for their snacks and also elaborate baths two times a day!

I remember my mom narrating many incidents. Once, when she was a small girl, they were all sitting in a group at night. No electricity in those days. Suddenly, she felt something slimy and threw it away, screaming in fright. The elders came with a torch and lights and found that it was a small snake. Immediately, someone was sent to a vaidyar with the news. He was an expert concluding whether the snake was poisonous or not and if it was poisonous, remove the poison from the body of the victim. He could come to a conclusion about the snake just by seeing the messenger who brought the news. Seeing this messenger, the Vaidyar declared that it was not a poisonous snake and gave some sacred ash to be adorned by her that night. It was very unbelievable, but we can't help but believe these things! In those days, there were no hospitals, antivenom injections, and no proper transport in those areas.

As I have already mentioned, my mom was a good storyteller and her stories about her childhood experiences went on and on. There, at Elapully, she had a favorite cousin called Rajammal. Mom used to say that she sang well. She was an excellent cook too and they always had a variety of goodies prepared and stored. She had two boys and two girls. One girl is one year older than me and one boy is my brother's age. My uncle Appammama's son Mohanettan later married Vijayedathy.

I remember going there as a young girl and staying with my mom. Vijayedathy and myself were very young and her sister, Vasanthedathy, was in charge of taking care of us. She made us bathe and brought two dresses of her sister's for us to wear. Our stay there was a sudden, unexpected plan, so I hadn't brought a change. Vijayedathy refused to wear that yellow dress, so her sister asked me whether I would wear it and agreed. She was given the other one. But I kept wondering why Vijayedathy refused to wear that and doubted whether she had vomited on that! I can bear anything but the smell of the vomit! Her sister was so nice and in the night, made our bed for us and kissed us goodnight. I started wondering why I did not have her as my own sister!

There were three houses- one, the main house where Rajammal valiamma & her family, her mom and bachelor uncle stayed. Aunty and uncle started staying there after my uncle's retirement. Then there was a pathayapura where their cousin, Lakshmikutty Valiamma and family lived. Then there was another one where her sister and family lived. In that house, there was one Shivaramankuttiettan who left all of us at a very young age.

My father was working at Kota (before he went to Bhutan) for some time. Shivaramankuttiettan got a job in Rajasthan as suggested by my father, but a few months after taking up that job, he developed Meningitis and passed away. I still remember getting the news and my mother falling sick at the news. Dr. Kesavan Nair had to come and treat her.

My next stay at Elapully was at the time of Vijayedathy's wedding. The wedding was at Palani and only after a couple of days was she taken to her husband's house at Palghat since they had to wait for an auspicious day and time. The next day of the wedding Vijayedathy and I decided to skip dinner because our stomachs were full. Her mom persuaded us to eat something but Vijayedathy said we would drink only Bournvita and we had that. Dinner was served. Soft idlis with sambar and chutney, other delicacies and payasam… all were spread on the table. The bridegroom, Mohanettan and the other family members sat for dinner. He couldn't find Vijayedathy anywhere, so he asked aunty. Then she broke the news that both of us had decided not to eat and had Bournvita. Mohanettan didn't allow it and called both of us and made both of us have dinner. Very reluctantly, we both had since our stomachs were full but later, I had to visit the toilet in the night! No attached toilet there. My mother had to accompany me with aunty leading us with a torch. I don't know what happened to Vijayedathy.

My mom had fond memories of the days she spent at Elappully with her cousins. She was very smart and intelligent, but not bold at all. She could argue with any one, speak logically, not pious at all but at the same time, scared of the unknown even though she claimed that she did not believe in ghosts!

From what she had told me about herself, I had gathered that she was a tomboy at school. Once, she was loitering on the school premises when she noticed an empty rickshaw. She made her friend sit on the rickshaw and dragged it around when the teacher caught her and reprimanded her. Another day. Some rehearsal was going on inside a room and only the participants were allowed inside. She was, however, not a participant, still she tried to get in and when it failed, tried to peep in through the window. These girls standing outside, eventually started talking and making a hell of a noise when the teacher in-charge scolded them. My mom got so angry that she closed the door and bolted it leaving everyone inside to find a way to come out. At last, someone opened the door and chased away those naughty girls. The gang leader was, of course, my mom.

My mom, on the violin, entertaining her sisters-in-law

Even though she was naughty, she was good at studies and talented too. Moreover, she was a sports person as well! Mom used to play the violin and could sing. I believe that there was a music troupe, not like today's. They sang only Carnatic music. Invariably, my mom mostly played the violin. She was good at badminton. Had she been of the present generation, she would have scaled great heights!

CHAPTER-8

Blacky and Princy and some snake tales

"There's no question that pets are a vital part of our families. They bring us joy, happiness, and unconditional love.....and we wouldn't have it any other way."

"Our pets are our family."

- Ana Monnar

I have mentioned our doggie, Princy. He was brought to us as a puppy. When he was very small, he used to litter the place whenever he liked, but once my uncle, Kuttyettan scolded him and gave him a tight slap. He whined and whined, but realized his mistake and stopped doing that. After that, whenever he wanted to ease himself, he used to make sounds or scratch the door. On our opening the door, he would go out. My other uncles were surprised to see such a lovable, obedient, house broken puppy at our house when they came on holidays.

In the night he was unleashed and he took pride in going around and barking at the slightest provocation. We could see him standing on the wall and hopping and barking at shadows and sounds. Even the neighbors felt safe when Princy barked! When he grew up, he started disappearing during mating season and coming back whenever he felt like doing so.

Sometimes he never barked at night, but made a friendly sound. That made us think that someone was trying to entice him to get access to our compound. One night my mother could sense something and she heard Princi's feeble whimpering which subdued and she could see torch light flashing and moving around that big house. My father was not there. My mom picked up courage and went upstairs to my uncle's room and alerted him. He came down, but by then, the thief must have escaped, hearing the voice of people. Uncle wanted to open the door and face the thief with a stick in his hand. He was robust and a six-footer, very bold, but mom pleaded with him not to open the door lest the thief might attack and hurt him. The next morning we were relieved to see Princy intact.

Once my brother's friend came home and while playing with the dog, it bit him. My mother was so worried that she immediately washed the wound with soap and water and tied it and sent him home with my brother instructing him to inform his father about what had happened. I think he was given only a tetanus injection. If this had happened now, I don't know what would have been the result!

I remember Devi's cousin getting bitten by a mad dog at Cherpulachery. She was rushed to Palghat and had to be given an injection around her navel for fourteen days. I was a little scared to go with mom to meet her. I hid behind my mom and observed her and wondered whether she might have got Rabies and whether I could expect an attack or bite from her! We can't say how the mind works. There is no dearth for imagination.

Anyway, once Princy disappeared and never returned .We all felt very sad and mom even asked the scavenger who was in charge of catching dogs in that area to go and check whether he was trapped and killed. In those days, according to corporation rules, pet dogs should have a collar. Since mad dog menace was increasing, scavengers were asked to capture stray dogs and these were killed. They were given some amount for each dog, so they removed the collar and took them away. We were told that our Princy was also caught like that! In those days no Maneka Gandhi and other activists. That was the sad end of our Princy! For days we couldn't sleep properly.

As for our Blacky, the cat. She was my good friend who very willingly shared my food which I offered under the table. She was a very tame cat. She initially had a bangle around her neck which was irritating her to the core. She patiently showed her neck when we tried cutting off the bangle. Eventually, the bangle had been removed by someone.

Blacky went on maternity leave whenever she chose to. She wouldn't be seen for some time. Then suddenly. One day she would come stealthily with her kittens. Our house was the main house where she felt very safe. It was very interesting and entertaining to watch her train the kittens to catch prey. She shook her tail very slowly and the kittens had to catch it. When the kittens grew up, they left. Again, Blacky could be seen sleeping under my feet, cuddled and if possible, sharing a bit of my blanket in rainy season.

One day, after Blacky returned with her kittens after her maternity leave, I was watching the whole family and their pranks. Suddenly, I noticed a small snake instead of Blacky's tail. I screamed and alerted my mom and others and the servant boy threw the snake out. Even though it was not a poisonous one, we were a little scared. Later, when Blacky disappeared from the scene, mom told Muthu the servant boy to put all the kittens in a gunny bag and leave them at a place far away from our house. Muthu did that. That night, when we all were sleeping, Blacky came with her catch, a dead rat. She called for her kittens, mewed miserably, searched for her kittens, but could not find them! How sad she would have been! The next day, again mom sent Muthu to bring the kittens back, but they could not be traced! Even animals show their affection to their babies and they become heartbroken if their babies are taken away from them!

Later also cats were coming to our house. Some used to deliver there; some used to bring the kittens from somewhere. That drama went on.

At this juncture I remember another thing. It was drizzling. I decided to go to Sakuntala's house for playing. When I reached her gate, I found one small snake slithering and going. It was a nonpoisonous snake. We had seen such snakes so many times. After some time I saw another one then another. Sakuntala and her siblings were sitting inside. Very cautiously, I went in when I was told that the maid had killed a snake and that's why the other snakes were coming. The maid sprinkled hing water to ward off the snakes. After some time, I went back home without playing. I was told that the snake's sound was heard by the other snakes at the time of killing it and they all came. I had never seen so many snakes slithering together! We don't know many things about nature!

Snakes are very scary and it is difficult for an ordinary person to distinguish between a poisonous and non-poisonous one. I really admire snake lovers like Vava Suresh who has a soft corner for snakes. In fact, snakes are very much necessary for balance in nature. Some even claim that they have divine characteristics. Anyway, if possible, let us not harm other creatures.

Once, our maid's daughter, Rajamani spotted two snakes winding on each other and 'dancing'. She said, "Don't look that side. It's not good to see snakes mating. It will bring bad luck." Whether it was the process of mating or the tussle of two male snakes to decide the winner, we didn't know. After that, I was scared to go to the backyard. I thought that that one might attack us.

Rajamani sometimes did foolish things without thinking of the consequences. The roads near our house were tarred when it became unusable. We could see a road roller parked there, some workers heating tar to lay on the road, small round pebbles and the activity was going on in full swing. Rajamani stealthily went there, cupped both the palms, scooped the fairly cool melted tar and stood up. She came to our house, tried to pour the tar somewhere and then to her bewilderment, knew that it wouldn't come out of the palm! She started howling and hooting. Her mother, Chinna and my mother scolded her like anything and then poured kerosene oil on the tar and after a tug of war with that black thing for a long time, she managed to save her palms. She whimpered for some more time and sighed every now and then and then got up. Only when we experience something drastic, will we know the reality.

CHAPTER-9

Manual scavengers

"In India, a man is not a scavenger by birth irrespective of the question of whether he does scavenging or not."

- Dr. B.R. Ambedkar

Lives of scavengers as I had seen!

In my childhood, I had seen manual scavengers. One woman used to come to our area. Like that there were many. Each one was allotted one or two particular areas. I am talking about the 1960s. The toilets were not the same as we have now. This woman used to come everyday to collect the excrement in a bucket! After collecting from many places, these scavengers took it to the PMC lorry to empty it there! The lorry headed somewhere to empty it! I am talking about the condition in Palghat.

The lives of these scavengers were miserable. Just for making money to make both ends meet, they were engaged in such activities. However, in the late 60s, the municipality gave notice for every household to build the present-day toilets (Indian toilets) and since it was government order people had to abide by it. The poor section of society was excluded from this. I think it was mainly to help those who were engaged in scavenging work. Constructing toilets was not like today's work. It was so elaborate. My mother's uncle was an engineer, so according to his instructions the plan was made and executed. I remember, there was one outside the house as we had earlier and another two, attached to the two bedrooms downstairs. However, there were scores of lower middle-class people who had not had this facility. The result was that they used the open space to defecate! Some used the toilets in different schools. In our school, only one toilet was cleaned and kept under lock and key. We children had to use the dirty ones! You can just imagine the plight of students in those days.

My uncles were happy to see the new toilets when they visited our house next. But at Cherpulachery, a village , such toilets were already constructed with some difference in technology. Today's generation can't imagine how people managed to live in such conditions. Now, there is luxury, modern bathrooms and toilets, ACs and what not! Still, no one is satisfied.

The scavenger woman of our area was one Karuppayi, if I remember correctly. I had seen her wearing clean clothes only on the 1st day of Karkidakam month (the Ramayana month). She went around all the houses with her small basket to collect food or money. By the time she reached our house, her basket would be filled with idlis and dosas and other food items and also money. My mom preferred to give money.

The previous evening our maid used to clean our house thoroughly and then sprinkle cow dung water and go around the house to disinfect the place. My mother then gave her a handful of coconut oil, some clothes and money. She would repeat, "chetta po, Sivothy va" meaning," go away evil spirits and we welcome the Goddess".

Ramayana month is supposed to be the lean month when people encounter scarcity of food and lack of work in those days. Now, the case is different. Anyway the whole of that month, people read Ramayanam every evening. That ritual is still followed by many families and there are food distribution in many temples and also Ramayam discourse the whole month.

Now that the availability of grains and pulses has improved, the middle class and upper-class people don't have scarcity of food, however, the workers find it a little difficult to make both ends meet since there is lack of work because of the unfavourable climatic conditions and also because of the boozing habit of the major breadwinners of the families. In the poverty-stricken families, not only men but women and children also had to work to make a living.

When I was a small girl, I had heard the fully drunk gents in the neighboring huts abusing their wives and beating them and the women crying and screaming at the top of their voices. It had become a routine in the nights! I wonder how the inmates lived without losing their mental balance. The women had to find some job as servants or at the construction sites and take care of the children. Most of the children did not go to school as they did not have the midday meal programme in school as we have it now.

The scavengers' lives were more miserable than this. It is sad to know that manual scavengers still survive in India! On one side, there are millionaires and people who overindulge in showy activities, some who revel at the cost of others, who don't even feel ashamed in begging and borrowing from others to show off infront of others and on the other side, there are people who moil and toil to help others without even thinking about their own safety! The tax evaders and hoarders come under the first category whereas the humiliated and poverty-stricken ones come under the second category. Even now, people litter places, water bodies and happily go away. The sight of the water bodies, impregnated with waste materials is a heartbreaking one. Who will clean up the place? We, the wrong doers should!

Why are there differences like this among human beings, I often wonder.

"Manual scavenging is the worst symbol of untouchability."

- National Advisory Council resolution

CHAPTER-10

Different outlooks

"Every house needs a grandmother in it."

- Louisa May Alcott.

The present scenario is entirely different from that of around 50-60 years back. In those days, most of the ladies in middle class and upper-class families chose not to go out and work. Here and there one could find teachers or very rarely, doctors. But nurses were more common. The ladies had to take care of the family and household work. However, they could pursue their talents to some extent. Many were good at painting, stitching, art and craft, singing etc.

My paternal grandmother was not well versed in these areas, but she was a very good housewife who was able to manage her home in a marvelous way. She was very pious and was the pillar of strength for the whole family. When young she had to marry a widower and lived with him and delivered six children. A very soft-spoken lady, granny had her own likes and dislikes. Her first daughter passed away at the time of delivery. In those days, ladies mostly delivered at home. There would be an experienced woman to help her at the time of delivery, but they could never handle a complicated situation. Going to the hospital was not common in those days.

My paternal grandfather became very sick after he lost his first daughter. Slowly he too passed away. My granny had to take care of the other children and manage the house and overcome her grief and she was able to achieve these. Instead of brooding over the past, she equipped herself and moved forward. You observe everyone around you. You can learn so many things from each one. Now-a-days, going into depression is very common. Something has to be done to strengthen our minds.

Her faith in God and her pious nature helped her time of sorrow.

My maternal granny (ammamma) did not have to face such severe problems even though her husband, my ammachchan, had been estranged from her. My maternal grandfather had been an advocate and had a flair for writing. He had worked as the sub editor of an English daily. He was articulate and an entertainer who enjoyed writing "Ottan Thullal", a Malayalam poetic art. He used to take ordinary topics to write these inorder to entertain small groups of people. None of these had been published. However, his 'diary' was published as "Rasakkatta" in Malayalam. In English, he published a "Worry Killer." After estrangement from my granny, he married another lady and had two children. He and the boys used to come to Cherpulchery to see my mom and us children. I have a vague memory of seeing them.

Ammamma had her strong father and mother to take care of her, so she didn't suffer loneliness or insecurity. In their generation, the oldies used to make decisions about their children's lives, not their children. The present generation prefers to take decisions on their own. But her life was also not totally problem free.

Ammamma had a small box with her to keep her needles and threads and a thimble and a small pair of scissors. She liked mending her dhotis and altering the pattern of her blouse. Apart from these she used to make small jasmine garlands for me to adorn my hair.

It was very soothing to see both my grandmothers. Both of them were fairly healthy till they passed away.

I found my ammamma very upset one day when she saw me come back from school panting and sweating! After the 10th results came, I went and collected my SSLC book from school. Sakuntala could go only at noon. After she came back, she sent word that I had to go back to school with the SSLC book for the headmistress was not sure whether she had signed my book. Without wasting much time, I went to school, clarified her doubt and returned.

I was a few yards away from my house when I noticed a man standing at the fence. When I was about to reach, I threw a cursory glance at him and he suddenly lifted his dhoti and displayed his nakedness. I was so scared .There was no one around. I screamed as though I saw a lion charging at me and turned and started running. After a few steps I turned back to see whether he was pursuing me. But then I noticed him turning the other side and hastily walking away. At the same time, my neighbour, an advocate, walked out of his house and started going in that direction. Seeing him, I bucked up courage and started walking fast to reach him so that he would help me. And I reached home. My parents were standing there waiting for me. I gasped and collapsed and asked for water. All of them were very scared. I narrated everything and my father went to the gate to see whether that man was there. But he had disappeared.

When our servant heard this, she said that many times she had seen such people and told me not to worry and get panicky. Later too, when we, friends were going together, we had seen my maniacs engaged in such exhibitionism!

My ammamma was a little worried that day. She was different from achamma. I had never seen her doing anything in the kitchen. The only thing I had seen her do was churning the butter milk. When I was smaller than that age, she used to wipe my hair with the bath towel after I took bath. Later, she started finding it difficult to do that since my hair had grown long. Her dinner was normally two chapatis and curry and a lotta of milk. When my uncles came to take her with them, I had seen her go with them in their cars. She did not have the habit of going to the neighbouring houses and gossipping. The only time she walked out with me was to Jayasree's new house when her father got a house constructed in the same street, at the end of the road.

However, my achamma was different. She was everywhere in the house, giving instructions to the servants, keeping an account of the rice the tenant had brought, making delicacies, arranging vishukani etc. whereas in my house, my mom, not my ammamma did all these things. I loved both my grandmas.

CHAPTER-11

Titbits

"Not everyone is your brother or sister in the faith, but everyone is your neighbor, and you love your neighbor."

- Timothy Keller

Our area, Koppam, was a place of wonderful neighbours. The ladies of the houses made casual visits to one another. Some of us went together to attend functions. If someone died in one house, food was provided to the inmates of that house by the people of the neighbouring houses.

There was one family in that area which was very pious. The man of the house, an advocate, went to Sabarimala with a group of people every year. Some years they conducted Ayyappan vilakku elaborately. Evening and night, food was provided for the neighbours. Young girls of the neighbourhood took talams (bronze plates filled with a lamp and flowers and other things) and walk in two lines in front of the panchavadyam troupe while they play on the five different instruments, and the decorated elephant. First, paalakkombu (a particular tree's branch) was brought.

The usual proceedings are the following. It may differ from place to place.

Three miniature temples are made with the trunk of the banana tree.

One is the main temple for Ayyappa, another one for Devi and the next one is for Vavar.

Vavar is supposed to be the Muslim brother of Ayyappa. Three oracles having different coloured attires go round these and dance to the tune of the song and instruments. There is another ritual called Tiriuzichil where the oracle comes near the people over there with a lighted thiri (wick). That is supposed to be very auspicious. All these are a sort of psychological treatment for the people gathered there. If I remember correctly, the oracles at last cut down the temples. The final ritual is kanal chattam. Ember is spread over a small area and the devotees walk through that bare foot! That is a sort of offering to the Almighty. I think that is the final ritual. Anyway, we all had witnessed all these. It becomes all the more relishing if one is with friends! We enjoyed all these, together. I remember, once this was conducted at our house at Cherpulcherry too. We, the cousins, had a gala time then.

At Palghat, the people of that house were not only pious, but lovers of classical music too. Radhamani amma, the lady of the house, was a singer too. There was a fine arts society. Musicians were invited every month to perform. Sometimes, Kadhakali or dance was performed. We were members of that club. Some musicians were accommodated at her house when they came to perform. Special cooks were arranged by her to take care of their menu. The most important thing is that she used to invite us, neighbors, to meet these artists and interact with them. I remember meeting D K Pattammal and a few others.

I feel such rituals and get-to-gethers have more value and meaning and that bind people together. Now-a-days people revel in just partying and boozing. Will that help anyone? No, not at all!

There was another interesting character in our locality. There was one I A Panicker, a very learned and talented retired man. He was the old IA and AS. After retirement, he settled down at Palakkad. We could see him going for a walk early in the morning in shorts and a hat and a walking stick. The enthusiastic Panicker was very systematic and he liked to organize a short 'Annual Day' of our area. In those days there were no resident associations. He used to organize music, dance and various other things. The highlight was the Sanskrit play. He used to choose people from various families of the neighbourhood. He used to make it grand and after the National Anthem, distributed snacks. He wanted to start a common kitchen, but that did not materialize. Anyway, I had heard that he made a tea distributing machine and tried to supply tea near Victoria College, but that too was short-lived. Anyway, our part of the Koppam area was a place of talented, intelligent literati, but all these people were born a little early!

Like this, at Palakkad we had a lot of entertainment. Likewise, at Cherpulachery too, there was scope for enjoyment. All these were entirely different from the entertainments and enjoyments of today. There were no sophisticated cinema halls, no mobile phones, no TVs, no discoes and not many clubs and eateries, still people could entertain themselves and find happiness! Today's generation may wonder what type of enjoyment that is. Just try to visualize that ambience and era. You will like it.

At Cherpulcherry at our family temple, every year there would be one "Thalappoli" during May. All family members get together at our ancestral house (an ettukettu). The ettukettu buildings have two "Nadumuttams", These are all old constructions.

We all used to go to that house in the evening and have an early dinner of rice porridge and a thick curry with green gram or some other pulse. It was called puzhukku.

I remember going for that thalappoli. After dinner, we went to the temple which was probably two furlongs away. There we young girls took thalam and walked with the decorated elephants and the drummers. There were halts in between, but we went round the temple. At one point of time, the rounding stopped and we went back to the house. We could take a short nap and then again we were woken up and taken to the temple to carry the thalam and go round the temple. By early morning the whole function ended and we all returned home, very sleepy and tired. We children slept and slept till we came out of that drowsiness. All these had a lot of significance in soothing the mind, boosting the energy.

Next, at Cherpulachery, in another temple, on the day of a function people get together. In the morning, Poothan and Thira would go to each and every house. They should be given something in cash or kind. I wonder whether all these art forms, if I can call it so, are dying down!

For many years, I got a chance to be part of such functions along with my cousins. Our outstation aunts and uncles did not come regularly. However, one year, Kutticheriamma and her second son, Kitchu were there. Kochammama was transferred to the border and these two were stuck at Cherpulachery. Kitchu was only 3 or 4 years old. School reopened and everyone started going to school. Poor Kitchu was getting bored at home till our cousins came back from school. But Kitchu was a smart, lovable boy who was the apple of everybody's eyes.

There was a dhobi called Cherona. She used to come and collect clothes from Ramavilas. Once a week she came normally, but since she was enamoured by the innocence and charm of Kitchu, she started coming every day to spend some time with him and entertain him. Days rolled by. Kutticherimma and Kitchu were getting ready to go to Kochammama.

Every month, at the beginning, achamma used to buy provisions from a nearby shop. She used to maintain an account book for that. That month, the account book disappeared. They searched everywhere, but no sign of the book. The shopkeeper was not very sure of the amount due nor was achchamma. She was in a real dilemma. One day they were having lunch. Kitchu had a small stool with a drawer. That was his favourite seat. His mom was adjusting the stool's position when its drawer opened, partially exposing the account book. She exclaimed and pulled the book out. Kitchu grabbed the book deftly and said that that was his possession which he had kept safely to take it with him when his daddy came to fetch him. He wouldn't leave the book even though everyone tried to convince him about the importance of the book. He exclaimed, "This is the book I am taking with me so that I can write letters to Cherona, the washer woman." Cherona was a fairly old lady with curly hair and plump in stature. She had her hair tied in a bun. Since Kitchu was getting bored when his cousins went to school, Cherona used to come and entertain him before collecting the soiled clothes for washing. She had the gift of the gab and could amuse this chit of a boy. He was very fond of her and used to wait for her after his work of watching the birds, running around and chasing the hens. Everyone burst out laughing.

Kitchu

Kochammama and family spent a few days at our house and a few days at Ramavilas. Kitchu was a little scared of Kuttyettan since his voice was very loud and he wouldn't tolerate any nonsense. Kitchu was in the habit of imitating all of us in a funny way and he would even say that all our faces looked crooked. Since he was a small child, we all enjoyed his performance and laughed, but if anyone asked him to imitate Kuttyettan, he would say that he was all good and his face was straight. He was scared that uncle might scold him! Before leaving Palakkad, after his leave Kochchammama and family always touched the feet of ammamma.

Even though Kochammama was in the military and looked very rough and tough, with his flourishing moustache, an authoritative voice, he was actually a very nice person who loved his people. He had certain peculiarities which made him different from others. This uncle never had any sensitivity towards fine arts like uncle Unnimama. The latter showed proclivity towards art at a young age, I believe. Instead of listening to the masters, he made a brilliant effort to draw lively pictures of them which got him into trouble. Complaints reached home sometimes. Sometimes, instead of going to school, he went to the Devi Studio to help him with photography. Anyway, his talents got him a job. Kochammama could never enjoy music of any kind. When the other family members were listening to the music concert of a renowned classical musician, he remarked bluntly," This sounds like a cat and a dog having a fight!"

This uncle rarely went out when he came on leave. He preferred to sit at home and relax with the family. We all were not like that. We liked to take a stroll down the road whenever possible. Once Kochammama had to go out and give a piece of his mind to the authorities at the EB office. One full day there was no electricity in our house. Every one hoped against hope that it would be restored very soon, but that did not happen. By evening uncle became very restless. He adorned his Military uniform and tiptoed into the electricity office with my brother escorting him. There, he asked for the officer in charge. Unfortunately, he had gone out to have a cup of tea. Uncle's wait was making him very uncomfortable. At last, slowly, the officer came. Seeing my boiling uncle, that too in Military uniform, he hesitated a little and then asked what he wanted very politely.

Twitching his moustache, Kochammama said, "From morning, we didn't have electricity in our house. There are small children as well as old people in our house. Why don't you restore electricity immediately? Do you want me to complain to the higher authorities and get you into trouble? If that shouldn't happen, do your duty. Restore electricity in that whole area before I reach home." The perspiring officer promised to do what he was asked to do and looked at him from head to foot, without missing the revolver and gave the necessary instructions to his subordinates. He and my brother walked back home and when they reached home, found everyone relaxed and smiling since electricity had been restored. Uncle was a man of action!

Appammama was slightly different from these two uncles. After Appammama settled down at Palakkad, we used to wait for him and his wife, Suseela valiamma to come and spend some time with us. They used to visit us once every fifteen days or so. Suseela valiamma sometimes felt lonely because they both were alone and they had servants who could take care of the house. One day Appammama asked mom whether I could be taken to stay with them for a month or so for holidays. He said he would bring Malini also from Elappully so that we could interact and play. And, Malini and I went to Appammama's house and stayed for a month, to the extreme happiness of Suseelavaliamma. Uncle took us for movies, bought us blouse pieces and aunty made the servants prepare delicacies for us for evening tea. Malini and I became friends there and we enjoyed talking and playing. He brought me back after our stay there. Appammama used to shout at people on the road if they did not obey traffic rules. He would put his head out, while driving and ask them, "Do you want to die? Where are you going in a hurry?" Otherwise, "If you can't control the bullocks, why should you drive a cart?" etc., to the greatest amusement of his co-passengers.

From the Post Office side, there were two ways to our house. One was in front of the LP school next to the big banyan tree which housed many birds. It's refreshing to walk that way listening to the chirping of birds, but we had to be cautious, otherwise we might be showered by bird droppings! It was disgusting. The Banyan tree had witnessed many things. I had always felt that if it could talk, it would have narrated many stories. Once my friend Meenakshikutty and myself were coming back from college when we found a healthy brown horse feeding itself on the grass given to it. It was happily farting and urine was flowing out as if from a hose. Unbothered about the people around watching and laughing and giggling at the sight, the stallion resumed relishing its food. People had seen a Zoophile wandering under that tree.

At around seven pm we had seen a coloured, sweetmeat cart going that way. It looked very attractive and sometimes, the cart came to our street too. It was pushed by a man and he rang a bell too to attract the attention of people.

At night, at a particular time, past midnight we used to hear a clanging sound from that side. There is no dearth of stories. People used to say that a big snake used to pass that way every night at that time making that sound. We had heard many stories and superstitions also spread like wildfire. Many stories were about Yakshis. Early in the morning, many girls or middle-aged women of the working class went out to the thickets to ease themselves since they didn't have toilets at home. Females were invariably, unhurt. Once, a man went, I believe and he happened to encounter a woman in her white dress. She stopped, looked at him and shyly asked for 'chunnambu.' The man stretched his hand, possibly with the intention of dragging her, but later, his people found not him there, but his dead body. Another story was that a white clad woman was walking early in the morning near the thicket when a man followed her. She turned and threw something at him and he fell unconscious. Later, when he woke up, he found himself infested with smallpox! I think people spread such stories just to protect women from the clutches of sex maniacs. Our maid's daughter, Rajamani, had a Pandora's box of stories like these.

The Banyan tree had witnessed many other things too. Chinna's mother Tayu used to work in our house. She had two granddaughters.

Her son divorced his wife and married another one. That lady had two boys. Tayu's son passed away soon and the burden of getting the younger girl married fell on her head. The first one was already married, but also became a divorcee soon. My mother helped her marry off the second girl. After that Tayu used to come home everyday and have lunch which my mom provided.

These people were living in small huts nearby. There, people of different huts and small houses got together to interact with each other in the evenings. The net result was that the first girl, the divorcee, fell in love with a man there. Her grandmother knew that. They were in two different communities. Their people would object tooth and nail if this marriage took place. They, however, decided to get married with the support of Tayu. In the darkness, when everyone was busy with their own work, Tayu and her granddaughter, walking under the Banyan tree, brought their brass vessels , covered them with some cloth and stored them in our house. My mother also supported them because she was very well aware of their condition. Even though the girl was working as a maid in some house, after the death of Tayu, she would be alone and would be exploited. My mother considered her safety too. One fine day, they both got married and they came to our house. Eventually, they took their brass vessels too from our house.

The man was apologetic, but mom said that there was nothing wrong in giving a life to a divorcee. She gave them high tea and they left happily and slowly they came and collected her vessels from our house. She later gave birth to two girls and they both were very studious and now they are leading comfortable lives, I believe. The girl was, however, ostracized from her community. Luckily, there was no honour killing.

Years rolled on and everything started changing. We all grew up, slowly one by one we all got married, some of us took up jobs. Many are scattered in different parts of the world. My parents shifted to Chennai. Till both of them passed away, we could meet them. They spent their time with Ettan and me and our families. At Ramavilas, first achamma passed away, then after some years, Devi's father.

Devi's mom went with Devi.

Fortunately, all these people in our family who passed away did not suffer in their final stages. I often feel that I was lucky to have been born in such a lovable family. There were some misunderstandings among a few at times, but that did not stop anyone from loving the others. Hope that the now living members will be able to meet together at some place.

We don't know what will happen after death, whether we will be born again, whether all of us will be part of the same family, whether we will be born on this planet. Hope everyone's journey will be peaceful!

I am reminded of the quote in Life After Life

"The beauty of life lies not in its perfection, but in its imperfections and the lessons they hold."

- Life After Life